AF673826

BLOOM

Olympiad ACE

A Comprehensive Practice Book

for School Olympiads & Talent Search Exams

MATHS

Class 4

by

Mohit Soni

Olympiad ACE

BLOOM

Bloom Cap Edu Ventures Pvt. Ltd.

Administrative & Production Office

'Ramchhaya' 4577/15, Agarwal Road, Darya Ganj, New Delhi -110002
Tele: 011- 47630600, 43518550

PRICE: ₹125.00

PO No. : TXT-59-T063301-02-25

Published by Arihant Publications (I) Ltd.

For further information about the books log on to
www.bloomcap.org

Follow us on

Preface

"Future belongs to those Who prepares for it today"

School Olympiads are National & International level competitions conducted by different Government, Non-Government & Educational Organisations with the purpose of making the children ready to face competitive exams. The challenging Questions asked in Olympiads motivate them to learn more & more and bring out the best result with improved academic performance. The Awards & Scholarship offered in Olympiads motivate children to aspire & strive for doing better and emerge out to be the best.

Maths Olympiads

Mathematics is an integral part of all competitive exams be it Aptitude or Commerce or Science. Maths Olympiads are meant to develop Mathematical aptitude in school students. They provide students with an opportunity to master their concepts and comprehend tricky questions effortlessly. Challenging Questions of Maths Olympiads encourage students to develop a logical approach to solve Mathematical Problems.

'Bloom Mathematics Olympiad Study Book Class 4' is a perfect resource to Study & Practice for Olympiad Exams and other National & State Level Talent Search Exams & Other Competitions.

Some Special Features of Bloom Maths Olympiad Study Books are;

- Chapterwise Exercises having different types of Objective Questions at par with the Olympiad Level.
- Detailed Explanation for each question.
- Olympiad Pattern Practice Sets at the end.

This book is prepared by Expert Panel with the utmost care, still if you have any suggestions regarding its improvement, then feel free to contact us at support@bloomcap.org. We will try to inculcate your suggestions in the further editions.

Contents

Chapter 01

Numbers

1. There are eighty six thousand four hundred seconds in a day. How else could this number be written?

(a) 80064 (b) 80640
(c) 86400 (d) 86404

2. Write 23456 in words.

(a) Twenty three thousand four hundred.
(b) Twenty three thousand four hundred fifty six.
(c) Twenty thousand four hundred
(d) None of the above

3. Which one of the following digits does not occur in the difference between the successor of 67854398 and the predecessor of 54677456?

(a) 1 (b) 3
(c) 2 (d) 4

4. A man shows his fingers as shown in the figure. It represents the roman numeral _____ .

(a) 5 (b) 4
(c) 6 (d) 2

5. Some roman numbers are given below. Use the sign '>, < or =' to fill the boxes and then choose the correct option that follow.

I.	LIV	☐	XCIX
II.	XLIV	☐	XLVI
III.	CCV	☐	XCV

(a) =, <, < (b) <, >, =
(c) <, <, > (d) >, <, >

6. The picture given below shows four different magazines. The numeral below each magazine is the total number of copies of the magazine sold last year.

MCCCLIII MCXXIII DXXIV DCCXLVIII

The number of copies sold in which magazine has 4 in tens place?

(a) All sports (b) Young people
(c) Teenage (d) Music time

7. What is the difference between the face value and place value of 9 in the number 26594325?

(a) 89991 (b) 9999
(c) 10999 (d) 89982

8. A teacher while teaching wrote some numbers as given below, in which all are same except one.

The one which is different, will be

(a) 100 ones (b) 10 tens
(c) 1 hundred (d) 100 tens

9. Three persons spent ₹ 1072, ₹ 260 and ₹ 128 to buy some household items. If the amounts spent were added, then how many tens are there in the total amount?

(a) 1 (b) 4
(c) 6 (d) 2

10. A number contains the digit 4 in it. Which of the following cannot be the number?

(a) 34 tens 47 ones (b) 42 tens 7 ones
(c) 41 tens 27 ones (d) 82 tens 22 ones

11. Jamal's clues about his mystery number are as shown in the box. What is Jamal's mystery number?

My number has

(i) 5 tens	(ii) 8 thousand
(iii) 2 ones	(iv) 6 ten thousand
(v) 0 ones	

(a) 58260 (b) 62850
(c) 68052 (d) 86520

12. Which abacus shows the correct representation of 9243?

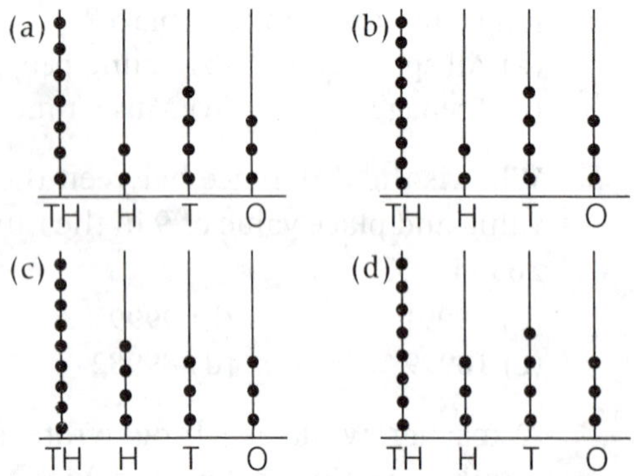

13. Two persons were having an amount of ₹ 435900 and ₹ 455500 respectively. What is the place value of '4' in the total amount of both the persons?

(a) 40 (b) 400
(c) 40000 (d) 400000

14. Who am I?

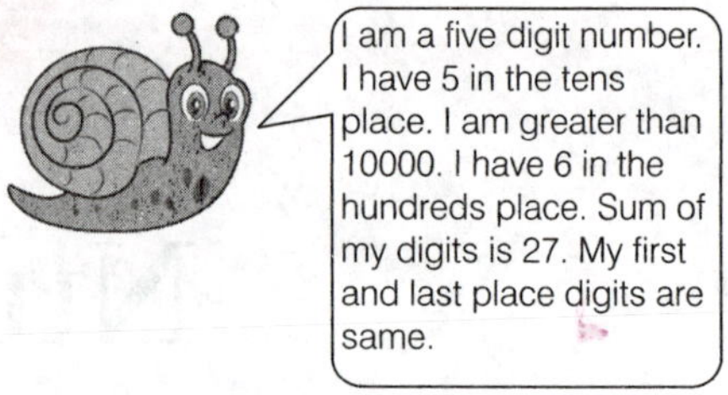

(a) 80658 (b) 70577
(c) 90858 (d) 20252

15. 596280 = 500000 + ☐ + ☐ + ☐ + 80 Which three numbers should be used to fill the boxes correctly?

(a) 90000, 6000, 200
(b) 60000, 9000, 200
(c) 9000, 60000, 200
(d) 9000, 6000, 20

16. Which number out of the given choices should be inserted in the box, so that the given series is in ascending order?

1743, 1898, ☐, 2098

(a) 1836 (b) 1899
(c) 1888 (d) 1829

17. Which of the following option shows the correct descending order.

(a) 87324 > 76284 > 76324 > 76423
(b) 52384 > 52834 > 25384 > 52348
(c) 57324 > 57234 > 43275 > 34275
(d) 57424 > 65324 > 56324 > 56432

18. Sonia reads some pages every month given in the table below. In which month, did she read the least number of pages?

Months	Number of pages
January	6916
February	6909
March	6876
April	6887

(a) January (b) February
(c) March (d) April

19. The population of Bolivia is 453400, which is rounded nearest hundred.
Find which of the following number could be the actual population of Bolivia.

(a) 4500321 (b) 453295
(c) 453364 (d) 4544892

20. Study the following statements and select the correct option.

Statement 1 : 5466 when rounded off to the nearest tens gives 5500.

Statement 2 : 41464 when rounded off to the nearest hundreds gives 41000.

(a) Statement 1 is true but Statement 2 is false.
(b) Statement 2 is true but Statement 1 is false.
(c) Both Statement 1 and Statement 2 are true.
(d) Both Statement 1 and Statement 2 are false.

21. Two children were playing a game using blocks with numbers written on them. A child asked his friend to form the smallest 5-digits odd number with the given blocks.

3	0	2	7	6

The number will be

(a) 02367 (b) 20367
(c) 30267 (d) 23076

22. The difference between the smallest and the largest 5-digit number formed by the digits 5, 4, 2, 6, 0 is

(a) 44964 (b) 62964
(c) 46956
(d) 62985

23. Match the following and choose the correct option.

A. 926543	(i) Smallest 5-digit number
B. 10000	ii) Place value of 2 is 2000
C. 962540	(iii) 100039 when rounded off to nearest 100
D. 100000	(iv) Successor of 926542

	A	B	C	D		A	B	C	D
(a)	(iv)	(i)	(ii)	(iii)	(b)	(ii)	(iii)	(iv)	(i)
(c)	(iv)	(iii)	(ii)	(i)	(d)	(ii)	(i)	(iv)	(iii)

24. Fill in the blanks and choose the correct option.

(i) 8 (ii) largest (iii) 13 (iv) 0
(v) smallest (vi) 2
(vii) cannot be determined (viii) 7

I. One crore is a/an ..... digit number.
II. The successor of largest 4-digit number is the ...... 5-digit number.
III. .... number has no roman numeral.
IV. Difference between the successor and the predecessor of a number is always ....

	I	II	III	IV		I	II	III	IV
(a)	(vi)	(ii)	(iii)	(vii)	(b)	(i)	(v)	(iv)	(vi)
(c)	(i)	(v)	(iii)	(viii)	(d)	(viii)	(ii)	(iii)	(vii)

25. State whether true or false and choose the correct option.

I. 6380 is 6400 when rounded off to nearest hundred.
II. Hindu Arabic number for Roman number CCXLV is 265.
III. Smallest 4-digit number that can be formed by using the digits 3, 5, 8, 0 is 0358.
IV. Sum of the smallest and largest 4-digit number is 10999.

	I	II	III	IV		I	II	III	IV
(a)	T	T	F	F	(b)	T	F	T	T
(c)	T	F	F	T	(d)	F	T	F	T

Chapter 02

Addition and Subtraction

1. Find the sum of below numbers.
35469, 23400, 10101

(a) 68970 (b) 69870
(c) 69780 (d) 60987

2. Select the correct match.

(a) XIV + V = 20 (b) X + XI = 19
(c) XI + XI = 21 (d) XI + XII = 23

3. Find the value of P and Q.

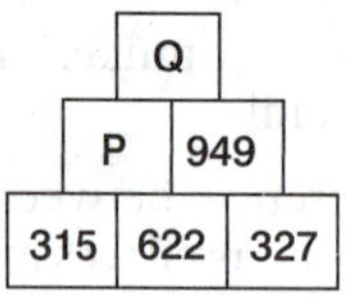

(a) P = 315, Q =2000
(b) P = 937, Q = 1886
(c) P = 500, Q = 1000
(d) P 949, Q = 937

4. Ria purchased a dress for ₹ 1457 and a pair of shoes of ₹ 643. What is the total amount she spent?

(a) ₹ 1457 (b) ₹ 2000
(c) ₹ 2100 (d) ₹ 1643

5. The given table shows the marks obtained by Radhika in five subjects out of 50. Which option is closest to the total marks of Radhika in all the five subjects?

Subjects	Marks
A	48
B	36
C	47
D	22
E	37

(a) 165 (b) 200
(c) 250 (d) 300

6. Tanvi bought a TV in exchange of an old fridge. The value of old fridge was ₹ 3250. If she had to pay ₹ 6329, then what was the cost of the TV that Tanvi bought?

(a) ₹ 6329 (b) ₹ 3250
(c) ₹ 9579 (d) ₹ 3079

7. John had 4 bags of pennies as shown below :

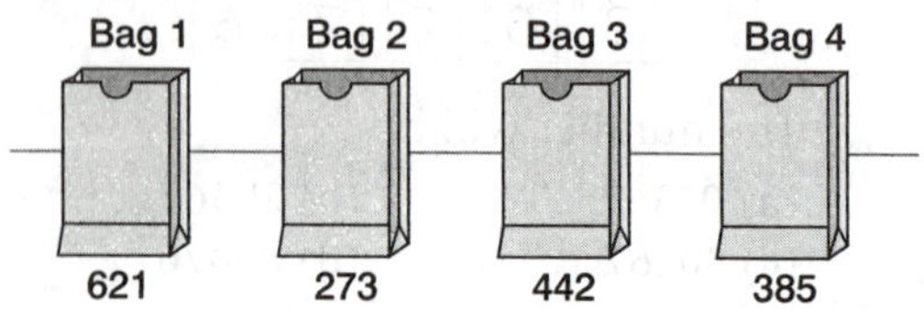

How many pennies John had in total when rounded off to nearest hundred?

(a) 1500 (b) 1700
(c) 1600 (d) 1800

8. Sonia goes 46 km North and returns back, then she goes 84 km East and return back. Find the total distance covered by her?

(a) 240 km (b) 860 km
(c) 260 km (d) 246 km

9. Find the minuend.

[?] − [5] = [95]

(a) 50 (b) 40
(c) 15 (d) 100

10. What is the value of 100 less than 3075?

(a) 1075 (b) 2075
(c) 2875 (d) 2975

11. D − XXX − LX is equal to

(a) 510 (b) 410
(c) 310 (d) 209

12. Find the value of $(P+T+Q)-(R+S)$.

```
  [P] 8  6  3 [T]
− 3  [S] 2 [R] 2
-----------------
   2  6 [Q] 2  1
```

(a) 12 (b) 10
(c) 3 (d) 9

13. Find the value of A, B, C and D.

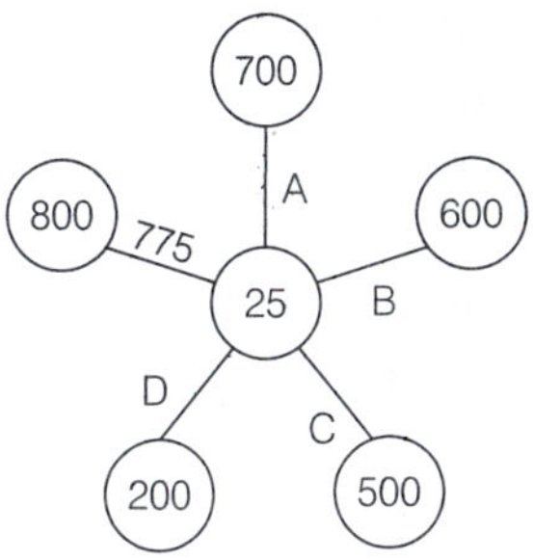

	A	B	C	D
(a)	775	675	375	475
(b)	675	575	475	175
(c)	675	575	475	375
(d)	375	475	375	875

Directions (Q. Nos. 14 and 15) Study the following pattern and answer the following questions.

```
  42859
− 14X26
-------
  27933
 −11Y9
-------
  26774
```

14. The value of X is

(a) 9 (b) 5
(c) 8 (d) 6

15. The value of Y is

(a) 1 (b) 3
(c) 5 (d) 2

16. Find the missing numbers.

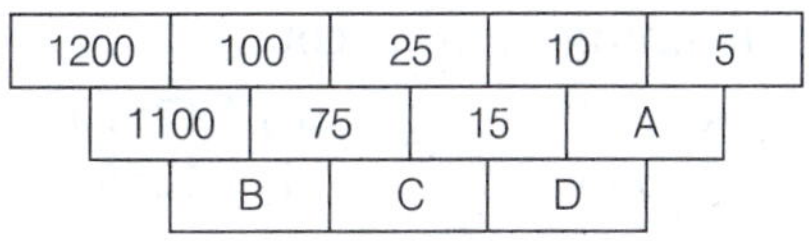

	A	B	C	D
(a)	5	1075	60	10
(b)	5	1025	60	10
(c)	5	1075	60	10
(d)	5	1075	60	1

17. The sum of 1264 and 427 is _____ more than the sum of 542 and 178.

(a) 471 (b) 971
(c) 1071 (d) 7991

18. The sum of two numbers is 17643. One of the number is 6689. Then, the other number is

(a) 24332 (b) 10954
(c) 65483 (d) 2219

19. 6598 plants were planted in Delhi by some school students on Environment day while 2593 plants were planted in Uttar Pradesh.

How many more plants were planted in Delhi than Uttar Padesh?

(a) 9191 (b) 4005
(c) 5824 (d) 6695

20. Cost price of a mobile phone is ₹ 3021 and that of another mobile phone is ₹ 2136. Estimate the difference in the cost of both the mobile phones.

(a) ₹ 885 (b) ₹ 905
(c) ₹ 880 (d) ₹ 775

21. Pawan open an account in bank with ₹ 4000. After one month he deposit ₹ 5276 in that account. Next month he again deposit ₹ 3274 in his account. After some days he withdraw ₹ 5000 from his account. Find the amount remaining in his account.

(a) ₹ 3274 (b) ₹ 17550
(c) ₹ 7550 (d) ₹ 12550

22. In a train, there are 482 passengers. 76 passengers get off the train and 46 passengers get in the train. How many passengers are there in the train?

(a) 652 (b) 452
(c) 537 (d) 153

23. A wholesale fruitseller bought 400 dozen fruits of which 67 dozen were oranges, 23 dozen were pears and the rest were apples. How many dozens of apples did he buy?

(a) 310 (b) 230
(c) 224 (d) 250

24. If

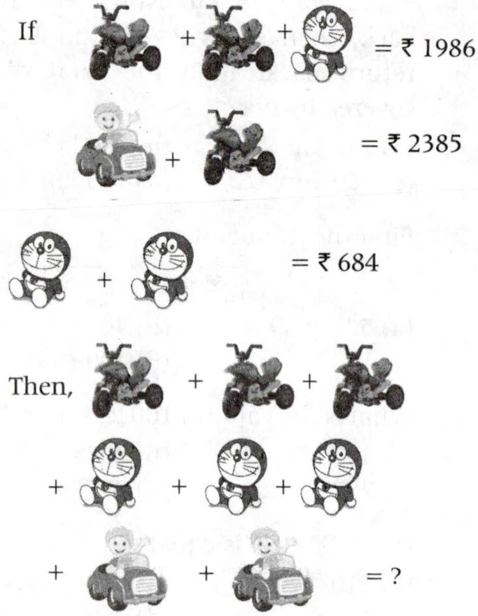

(a) ₹ 6618 (b) ₹ 5483
(c) ₹ 6495 (d) ₹ 4382

25. State 'T' for true and 'F' for false for the given option.

I. 97 + 87 + 77 equals to 263
II. We use addition when we find how many things are left.
III. 43496 – 27999 = 15497
IV. Subtraction is used to find out the total amount.

III III IV
(a) FF T F
(b) TT F T
(c) FT F T
(d) TF T F

Chapter

03

Multiplication and Division

1. Which of the following figure represents 3×4?

(a) 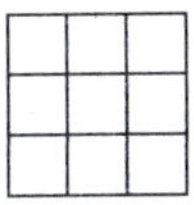

(b) 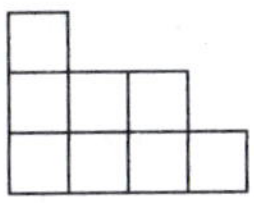

(c) 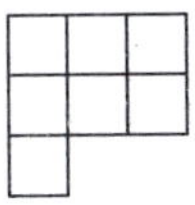

(d) 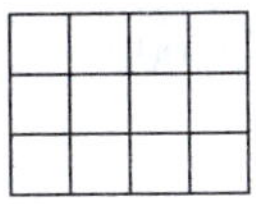

2. If there are five pearls in each Jewellery box. Then solve the problem.

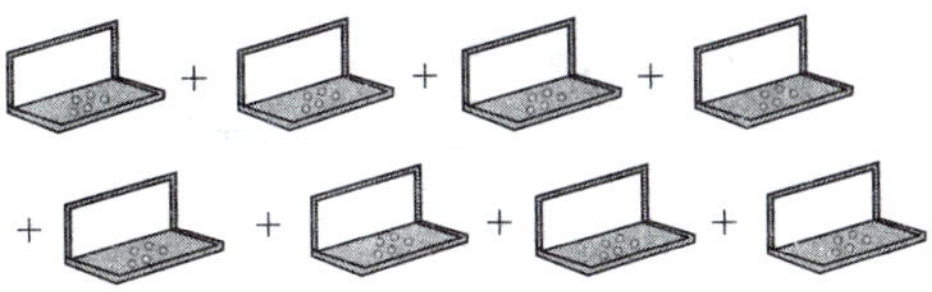

= — × — =

(a) $5 \times 8 = 40$
(b) $5 \times 9 = 45$
(c) $5 \times 10 = 50$
(d) $5 \times 10 = 10$

3. Fill in the blank spaces.

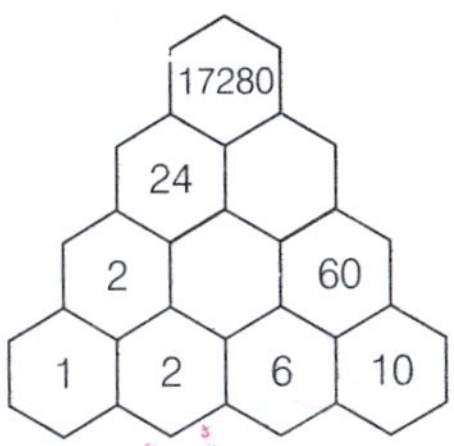

(a) 12, 240
(b) 24, 120
(c) 12, 720
(d) 60, 24

4. Find out the missing number.

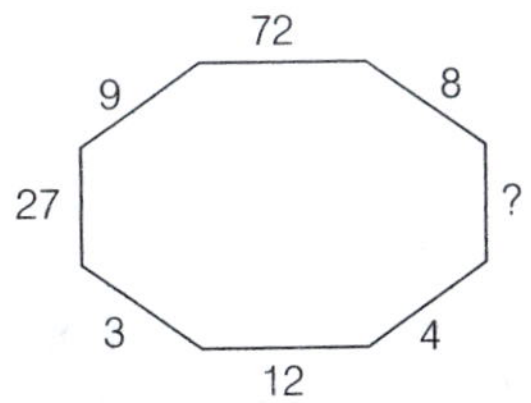

(a) 96
(b) 32
(c) 24
(d) 48

5. What is the product of all the numbers on a telephone keypad?

(a) 158480
(b) 159450
(c) 159480
(d) 0

6. Namita is playing a game in which she multiplies some numbers and get the product. Among the following, choose the option which does not have the product equal to 1144.

(a) 23×18
(b) 52×22
(c) 44×26
(d) 104×11

7. Aryan has 132 tickets. Each ticket can be used by 6 people. How many people can use the tickets?

(a) 610
(b) 792
(c) 685
(d) 22

8. A badminton court has 72 rows with 50 seats in each row. How many seats are there in the court.

(a) 3000 (b) 4600
(c) 3200 (d) 3600

9. Sahil, Johny, Devansh and Sonal have 120 play cards each. How many cards do they have in all?

(a) 360 (b) 420
(c) 480 (d) 580

10. In a grazing field, there are 60 goats, 30 deers and 10 children. How many legs are there in the field?

(a) 400 (b) 200
(c) 380 (d) 480

11. Cody is playing a game of darts. The dart board is divided into 3 sections having different points written on it. The score of Cody is the sum of the points he acquires after throwing 3 darts on the board. Which of the following cannot be the score of Cody?

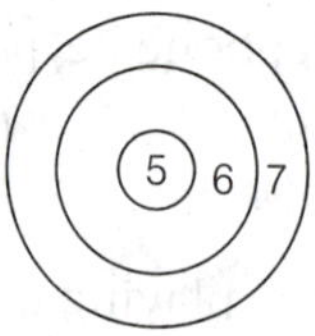

(a) 15 (b) 18
(c) 21 (d) 23

12. Martin and Louisa bought new sticker books. Martin put 4 stickers in his book everyday and Louisa put 6 stickers in her book everyday. How many stickers will Martin have when Louisa has 30 stickers in her book?

Days	Martin	Louisa
1	4	6
2	8	12
3	12	18

(a) 16 (b) 20 (c) 24 (d) 36

13. Fill in the blanks in reference to the given image.

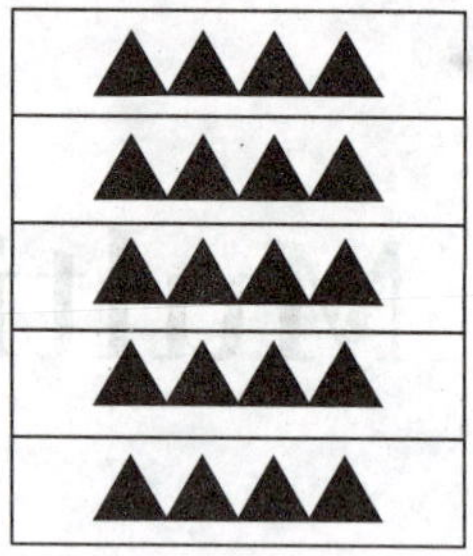

☐ ÷ ☐ = ☐

(a) $20 \div 5 = 4$ or $20 \div 4 = 5$
(b) $5 \div 20 = 4$ or $5 \div 4 = 20$
(c) $2 \div 10 = 20$ or $4 \div 5 = 20$
(d) $5 \div 20 = 4$ or $4 \div 20 = 5$

14. Complete the pattern.

_____ $\div 13000 = 2$
$26000 \div 1300 =$ _____
_____ $\div 130 = 200$
$26000 \div 13 = 2000$

(a) 26000, 20, 26000 (b) 2600, 2, 26000
(c) 20, 260, 26000 (d) 200, 2000, 2600

15. Find the value of $(L + M + N) \div P$.

```
12 ) 93795 ( 7[L]1[P]
     84
     ×[M]7
      9 6
     × 1 9
       1 2
      ×[N]5
        7 2
        × 3
```

(a) 5 (b) 4
(c) 2 (d) 1

16. Arnab has 72 cows on his farm. The number sentence below can be used to find the number of horses, h, Gary has.

$$72 \div h = 6$$

How many horses does Gary have?

(a) 12 (b) 466
(c) 78 (d) 432

17. There are 534 burgers which are to be packed. 6 burgers can be packed together in 1 packet. How many packets will be needed in all?

(a) 89 (b) 62
(c) 88 (d) 92

18. There are 5 friends and 13 mangoes. If the mangoes are divided equally among the students, how many mangoes will each friend get and how many are left?

(a) 2, 3 (b) 3, 2
(c) 2, 4 (d) 4, 3

19. Aman was asked to verify the answer of the given problem. What expression should he use to obtain the dividend again?

$$7\overline{)188}\quad 26$$

Remainder = 6

(a) $(6\times26)+7$ (b) $(26\times7)+7$
(c) $(7+26)\times6$ (d) $(7\times26)+6$

20. Nitu and Raj decided to sell bicycles. They have 27 bicycles in total. Both sold equal bicycles. Find out how many bicycle(s) will be left after selling?

(a) 2 (b) 1
(c) 3 (d) 0

21. Match the following :

Column-A	Column-B
A.  281 ÷ 12	(i)  Quotient-1193 Remainder-6
B.  8357 ÷ 7	(ii)  Quotient-23 Remainder-5
C.  7468 ÷ 5	(iii)  Quotient-191 Remainder-7
D.  1726 ÷ 9	(iv)  Quotient-1493 Remainder-3

Codes

	A	B	C	D
(a)	(ii)	(iv)	(iii)	(i)
(b)	(ii)	(i)	(iv)	(iii)
(c)	(iii)	(iv)	(i)	(ii)
(d)	(iv)	(iii)	(i)	(ii)

22. State 'T' for True and 'F' for False for the following statements.

(i) $720 \div 720 = 0$ (ii) $0 \div 47 = 0$
(iii) $8000 \div 2 = 4000$

(a) F, T, T (b) T, F, T
(c) T, T, F (c) F, F, T

23. Choose the correct option which makes the given statements true.

I. $94\times6 \,\square\, 6\times94$
II. $13\times9+6 \,\square\, 6\times9+13$
III. $0\div83 \,\square\, 83\div1$

(a) >, =, = (b) >, <, <
(c) =, >, < (d) =, <, =

Chapter 04

Multiples and Factors

1. Which number is the factor of every number?
(a) 1 (b) 0
(c) Number itself (d) None of these

2. 72 has _____ factors.
(a) 10 (b) 4
(c) 8 (d) 12

3. How many multiples of 20 are there between 10 and 190?
(a) 7 (b) 9
(c) 8 (d) 6

4. Some numbers are shown below :

1, 3, 9, 18, 15, 45, 24, 27, 30, 71

Which of the three numbers shown above are multiples of 9?
(a) 1, 3, 9 (b) 18, 45, 24
(c) 15, 45, 24 (d) 9, 18, 45

5. Mother gave 12 Apples to the Son and asked him to arrange them in 3 Basket under some conditions like
A. All Apples to be used.
B. Each Basket must have the same number of Apples.
This activity will help the children to understand the concept of
(a) Addition
(b) Subtraction
(c) Multiples and factors
(d) Measurements

6. Figure below shows the prime factors. Then, the value of x is

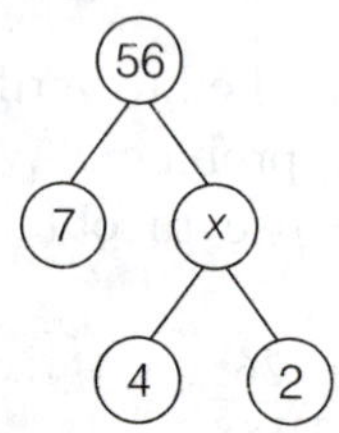

(a) 8 (b) 7
(c) 9 (d) 5

7. I am a factor of 45. I am single digit odd number. I am also a factor of 54. What am I?
(a) 7 (b) 9
(c) 5 (d) 11

8. Fill in the blanks and choose the correct option.

(i) 6	(ii) 4
(iii) 2	(iv) 8
(v) 9	(vi) 1
(vii) 7	(viii) 3

I. .... is the smallest odd prime number.
II. A number having more than .... factors is called composite number.
III. .... is neither a prime number nor a composite number.
IV. The numbers having factors 2 and 3 have factor .... also.

	I	II	III	IV		I	II	III	IV
(a)	(viii)	(iii)	(vi)	(i)	(b)	(iii)	(ii)	(vii)	(iv)
(c)	(vi)	(iii)	(iv)	(viii)	(d)	(ii)	(i)	(vi)	(v)

9. I. X has 2 more factors than 10 has.
II. X and 10 have 2 common factors.
What is the smallest possible value of X?
(a) 12 (b) 6
(c) 8 (d) 15

10. Anna collected 8 water bottles. Raj collected twice as many.
How many water bottles did Raj collect?
(a) 24 (b) 16
(c) 8 (d) 4

11. Use the equation given below to answer the question.

$$14 \times 3 = 42$$

Which statement correctly interprets the expression?
(a) 42 is 3 more than 14.
(b) 14 is 3 more than 42.
(c) 14 is 3 times as many as 42.
(d) 42 is 3 times as many as 14.

12. In the century (1900-1999), the year which is closest to 21st century and divisible by 2 and 5 both is
(a) 1999 (b) 1990
(c) 1995 (d) 1998

13. X is a number. X tells I am both factor and multiple of myself. Which one of the following is X?
(a) 1 (b) 5
(c) 7 (d) All of these

14. A number is between 20 and 30. It is also a multiple of 4. When it is divided by 8, there is no remainder. What is the number?
(a) 20 (b) 24
(c) 28 (d) 32

15. Subtract the sum of the 6th multiple of 7 and the 3rd multiple of 9 from the 11th multiple of 12. The result is
(a) 60 (b) 50
(c) 63 (d) 70

16. The smallest number which is a common multiple of 6 and 8 but is not a multiple of 9. When added to 7 fives gives the result
(a) 80 (b) 60
(c) 59 (d) 65

17. Nisha bought following books from the market which has price written below them. The price of which book is a multiple of 3?

(a) Maths Olympiad
(b) English Olympiad
(c) Computer Olympiad
(d) Science Olympiad

18. Four students made some statements regarding the numbers given below :

80 17 11 24
40 2 48 84

Max There are only 4 multiples of 8.
Jeniffer Every number is a composite number.
Rocky (40, 11) are coprime numbers.
Anjie All the numbers are not an even. number

Which one of the following made incorrect statement?
(a) Max (b) Jeniffer
(c) Rocky (d) Anjie

19. Which number am I?

I. I am a 2-digit even number.
II. I am a common multiple of 6 and 7.
III. I have a total of 8 factors.

(a) 43 (b) 35
(c) 42 (d) 84

20. Find the sum of (3rd multiple of 11) and (the difference between common factors of 8 and 10).

(a) 42 (b) 36
(c) 34 (d) 32

21. Raghav has the calendar for the month of January in which he has chosen a date for holiday. The date is such that it is a multiple of 7. Also, HCF of the date chosen and the number 24 is 2. What is the date chosen by Raghav?

JANUARY						
Sun	Mon	Tue	Wed	Thu	Fri	Sat
						1
2	3	4	5	6	7	8
9	10	11	12	13	14	15
16	17	18	19	20	21	22
23	24	25	26	27	28	29
30	31					

(a) 7 (b) 14
(c) 21 (d) 28

22. During summer months, one ice-cream truck visits Jeanette's neighbourhood every 4 days and another ice-cream truck visits her neighbourhood every 5 days. If both trucks visited today, then after how many days will both trucks visit on the same day?

[**Hint** Find the LCM of 4 and 5]

(a) 20 (b) 40
(c) 50 (d) 10

23. Here are steps given to find the greatest number of four digits which is divisible by 15, 25, 40 and 75. Identify the correct order of following steps.

I. On dividing 9999 by 600, the remainder is 399.
II. Greatest number of 4 digits is 9999.
III. LCM of 15, 25, 40 and 75 is 600.
IV. Number is $(9999 - 399) = 9600$.

(a) III I II IV (b) II III I IV
(c) III II IV I (d) II I III IV

24. State true or false and mark the correct answer.

I. Two numbers which have only one common factor are called coprime numbers.
II. 3 is the least prime number.
III. LCM of two prime numbers is always their product.
IV. The LCM of any two or more numbers cannot be less than any one of them.

	I	II	III	IV		I	II	III	IV
(a)	T	T	F	F	(b)	T	F	F	T
(c)	T	T	T	F	(d)	T	F	T	T

25. Match the following statements and mark the correct option.

I. LCM of 15 and 30	(i) 6
II. LCM of (8, 16)	(ii) 27
III. Sum of the factors of 2 and 15	(iii) Factor of 64
IV. HCF of 24 and 6	(iv) 30

I II III IV
(a) (i) (iii) (iv) (ii)
(b) (iv) (iii) (ii) (i)
(c) (iii) (ii) (i) (iv)
(d) (iv) (iii) (i) (ii)

Chapter 05

Fractions

1. Which shape does not show one-quarter shaded?

(a) 

(b) 

(c) 

(d) 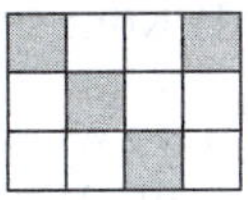

2. Select the image from the given options which has the same fraction of unshaded portion as the fraction of the shaded portion of the image below.

(a) 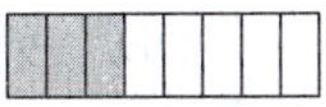

(b) 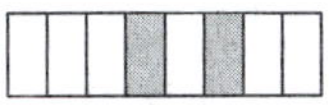

(c) 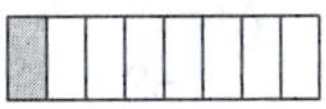

(d) 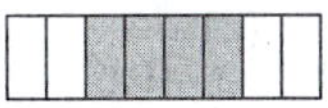

3. How many shaded triangles must be unshaded so that $\frac{2}{4}$ of the given figure is shaded?

(a) 1 (b) 3
(c) 4 (d) 2

4. What fraction of the letters of the given word has curved line?

E D U C A T I O N

(a) $\frac{5}{9}$ (b) $\frac{7}{9}$

(c) $\frac{4}{9}$ (d) $\frac{2}{9}$

5. Given a matrix below which shows two sets of fraction. Each fraction in Ist group is paired with its equivalent fraction in IInd group. Choose a method which should be used to convert the fraction into its equivalent form.

Ist group	$\frac{26}{65}$	$\frac{104}{117}$	$\frac{91}{143}$
IInd group	$\frac{2}{5}$	$\frac{8}{9}$	$\frac{7}{11}$

(a) Add 24 to both numerator and denominator.
(b) Subtract 13 from both numerator and denominator.
(c) Divide numerator and denominator by 13.
(d) Multiply numerator and denominator by 15.

6. The horses of four cowboys got mixed up. Using conversion of fraction, match the horses with their correct owner.

I.  $\xrightarrow{\frac{56}{9}}$ (i)  $\xrightarrow{4\frac{1}{9}}$

II.  $\xrightarrow{\frac{37}{9}}$ (ii)  $\xrightarrow{2\frac{5}{9}}$

III.  $\xrightarrow{\frac{23}{9}}$ (iii)  $\xrightarrow{4\frac{7}{9}}$

IV.  $\xrightarrow{\frac{43}{9}}$ (iv)  $\xrightarrow{6\frac{2}{9}}$

	I	II	III	IV
(a)	(iii)	(ii)	(i)	(iv)
(b)	(iv)	(i)	(ii)	(iii)
(c)	(ii)	(iii)	(iv)	(i)
(d)	(ii)	(iii)	(i)	(iv)

7. What is the value of x, so that the sum of fractions in the diagonal is same?

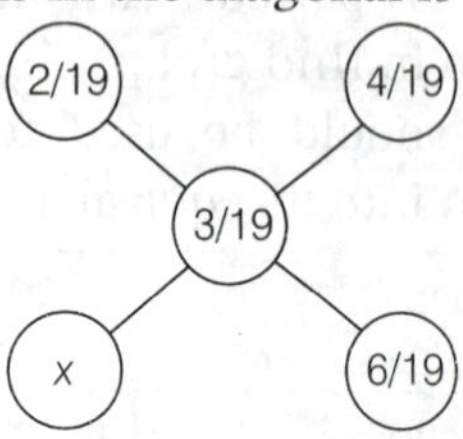

(a) $\frac{5}{19}$ (b) $\frac{7}{19}$
(c) $\frac{4}{19}$ (d) $\frac{8}{19}$

8. What is the value of $(Q-P)$?

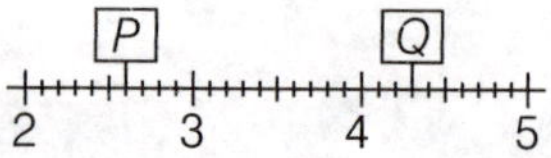

(a) $\frac{69}{12}$ (b) $\frac{17}{10}$
(c) $\frac{17}{12}$ (d) $\frac{54}{10}$

9. If $\frac{7}{X}-1\frac{3}{10}=\frac{1}{10}$, then find the value of X.

(a) 1 (b) 4
(c) 3 (d) 5

10. If $3\frac{3}{4}+2\frac{5}{6}=x\frac{y}{z}$, then find the vale of x, y and z.

(a) $x=6$, $y=12$, $z=7$
(b) $x=12$, $y=7$, $z=6$
(c) $x=6$, $y=7$, $z=12$
(d) None of the above

11. There were 15 frogs on a log. 11 hopped away. What fraction of the frogs left behind?

(a) $\frac{11}{15}$ (b) $\frac{4}{11}$
(c) $\frac{4}{15}$ (d) $\frac{15}{4}$

12. What fraction of alphabets are made of only straight lines?

(a) $\frac{15}{26}$ (b) $\frac{10}{26}$
(c) $\frac{7}{26}$ (d) $\frac{18}{26}$

13. Neha filled one-fifth of a jar with milk and two-fifth with water. What part of the jar is empty?

(a) $\frac{4}{5}$ (b) $\frac{2}{5}$
(c) $\frac{1}{3}$ (d) $\frac{1}{4}$

14. Following table shows the match routine of 4 players :

Players	Win	Lost	Matches played
A	4	6	10
B	3	3	6
C	5	7	12
D	8	2	10

Which player won exactly half the matches he played?

(a) *A* (b) *B*
(c) *C* (d) *D*

15. If A + B + C $=\frac{3}{4}$, A + B $=\frac{1}{3}$, then what is the value of C?

(a) $\frac{1}{12}$ (b) $\frac{5}{12}$
(c) $\frac{2}{11}$ (d) $\frac{1}{9}$

16. Shalini ate $\frac{1}{9}$ apples on tuesday, $\frac{2}{9}$ apples on wednesday and same on thursday. The fraction of apples left with her will be

(a) $\frac{4}{9}$ (b) $\frac{5}{9}$
(c) $\frac{1}{9}$ (d) $\frac{2}{9}$

17. The regular price of a meal is ₹ 84. If a coupon is available, how much will the meal price?

$\frac{3}{4}$ of coupon

(a) ₹ 21 (b) ₹ 63
(c) ₹ 45 (d) ₹ 70

18. The sum of unshaded fraction of 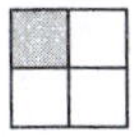 and  is ________ .

(a) $\frac{3}{4}$ (b) $1\frac{1}{2}$
(c) $2\frac{3}{2}$ (d) $1\frac{3}{4}$

19. Nishant bought $3\frac{6}{12}$ kg of sugar. He bought $\frac{1}{2}$ kg more sugar than Aman. How much sugar did Aman buy?

(a) 3 kg (b) 12 kg
(c) $1\frac{2}{6}$ kg (d) 9 kg

20. If  +  +  $=\frac{17}{12}$,  +  $=\frac{7}{6}$ and  −  $=\frac{5}{12}$, then what is the value of ?

(a) $\frac{1}{3}$ (b) $\frac{2}{3}$
(c) $\frac{3}{4}$ (d) $\frac{5}{3}$

21. There were 2000 males and 2500 females in a stadium. After 2 h, $\frac{2}{10}$ of females and $\frac{2}{5}$ of males left the stadium. How many persons were in the stadium after 2 hours?

(a) 2200
(b) 3600
(c) 3200
(d) 4000

Chapter

06

Measurements

1. The correct measure of the object to nearest millimetre is

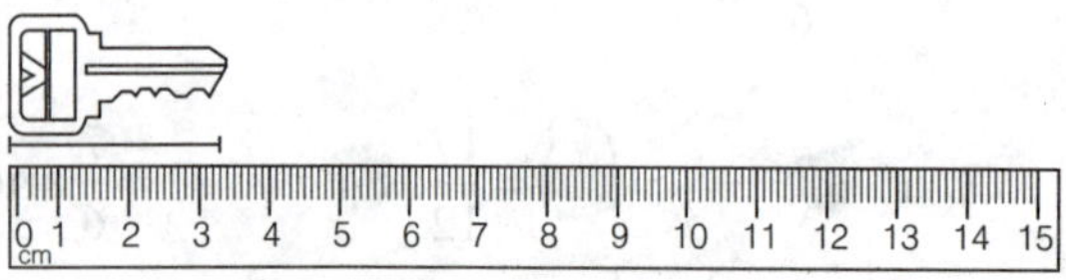

(a) 3 cm 4 mm (b) 3 cm 2 mm
(c) 3 cm 3 mm (d) 3 cm 5 mm

2. If each part on the number line is of 1 cm.

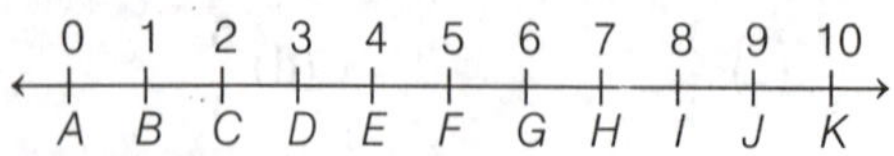

Then, sum of $AD + EF + HJ$ is equal to
(a) AF (b) DJ
(c) CG (d) EJ

3. A horse(s) height is measured in a unit called hand. A hand measures 4 inch. What is the height of a horse that measures 14 hands?

(a) 36 inch (b) 46 inch
(c) 56 inch (d) 66 inch

4. Aaron is going to his grandma's house. The distance between Aaron's and his grandma's house is as shown below. Due to wear and tear of the road, Aaron has to take the long route which is about 9.2 km. How much more distance Aaron has to travel in order to reach his grandma's house?

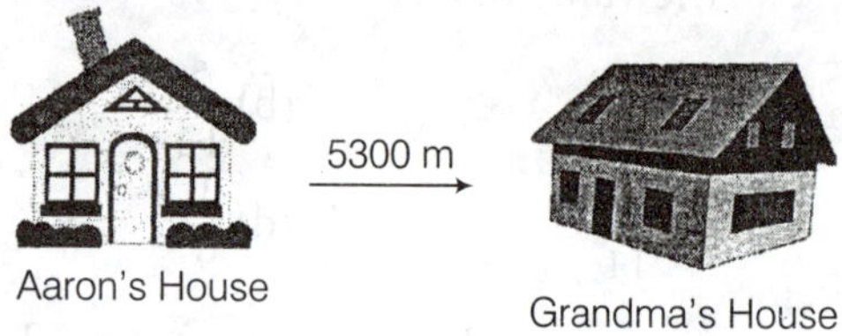

(a) 2.7 km (b) 3.9 km
(c) 4.8 km (d) 4.5 km

5. If the length of rope needed to make border X is 16 cm, then the length of rope needed for border Y.

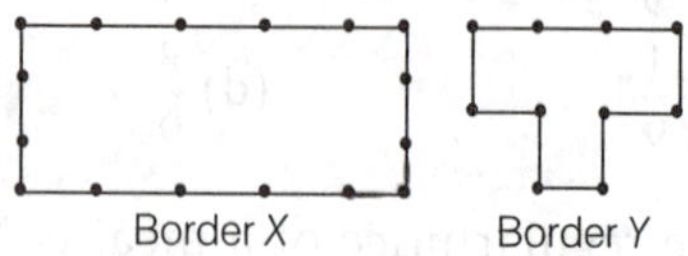

(a) 9 cm (b) 12 cm
(c) 10 cm (d) 13 cm

6. Kelsey's pencil box is 16 cm long. Hanna's pencil box is 4 cm shorter than Kelsey's. Mark's pencil box is 2 cm longer than Hanna's. How much long is Mark's pencil box?

(a) 12 cm (b) 14 cm
(c) 10 cm (d) 16 cm

7. Smith is taking part in an olympic race. The length of each of his step is given in the figure. Calculate how many miles can he run, if he took 20000 steps in the race? (given, 1 mile = 1.6 km)

(a) 9.468 miles (b) 9.32 miles
(c) 9.375 miles (d) 10.459 miles

8. A bridge is 600 m long and a truck is 5 m long. How many trucks can stand on this bridge, if the trucks stands with a gap of 1 m?

(a) 150 (b) 1920
(c) 100 (d) 130

9. A gift 38 cm long is to be wrapped with a wrapping paper. The length of wrapping paper is 64 cm. A margin of 5 cm on each side is to be taken for folding purpose. How much length of wrapping paper will be left after wrapping the gift?

(a) 21 cm (b) 16 cm
(c) 26 cm (d) 20 cm

10. Fill the missing sign and choose the correct option.

I. 8 ☐ 1000 g = 8 kg
II. 900 g ☐ 100 g = 1 kg
III. 4000 g ☐ 4 = 1 kg
IV. 780 g ☐ 280 g = 0.5 kg

(a) ×, +, ÷, − (b) ×, ÷, +, −
(c) ÷, ×, +, − (d) ÷, +, − +

11. The given diagram shows a weighing balance. 1st pan consists of weights worth 750 g and 2nd pan consists of 2 kg. How much weight is needed to add to 1st pan, so that the scales become balanced?

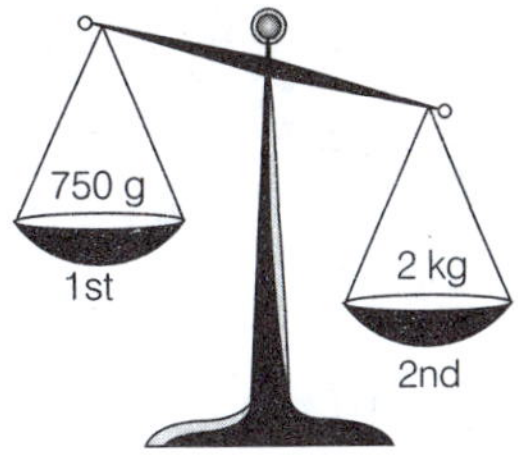

(a) 1250 g (b) 1000 g
(c) 1500 g (d) 1325 g

12. The weight of 3 books and a puppy is 12 kg. What is the weight of a book?

(a) 6 kg (b) 2 kg
(c) 4 kg (d) 5 kg

13. If  +  = 20 g

 +  +  = 46 g

 +  = 24 g

Then, the weight of  is

(a) 10 g (b) 6 g
(c) 12 g (d) 8 g

14. Which of the following options is Incorrect?

(a) 2 L 125 mL = 2125 mL
(b) 4 L 50 mL = 4500 mL
(c) 3 L 25 mL = 3025 mL
(d) 5 L 25 mL = 5025 mL

15. The correct arrangement of the following items in order to which holds the least capacity to most will be

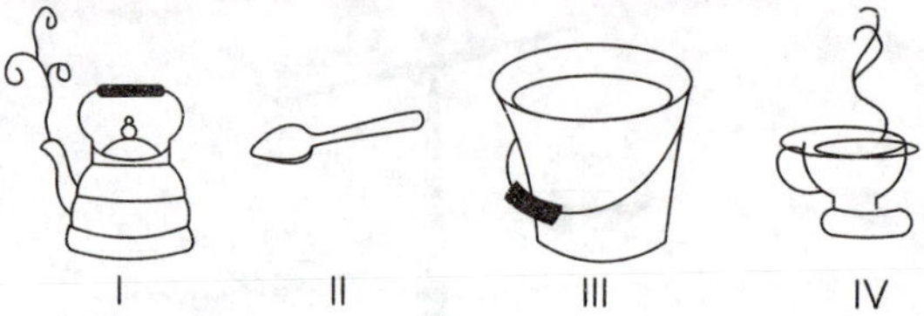

(a) II < I < III < IV
(b) II < IV < III < I
(c) II < I < IV < III
(d) II < IV < I < III

16. Which of the following should not be measured in litre or millilitre?

orange juice, petrol, potatoes, milk

(a) Orange juice (b) Petrol
(c) Potatoes (d) Milk

17. Moishe has a can of lemonade containing 400 mL. He drinks 1/4 of it. How much lemonade is left?

(a) 200 mL (b) 100 mL
(c) 300 mL (d) 250 mL

18. A doctor has syrup bottle which is to be given equally to the patients as shown in the diagram.

How much syrup will be given to each patient?

(a) 90 mL (b) 82 mL
(c) 85 mL (d) 63 mL

19. Krista has 1.5 kL of water in a tank. To empty the tank, she took a 125 L bucket and started watering the plants.
How many buckets will it take to remove all the water from the tank?

(a) 15 (b) 18
(c) 20 (d) 12

20. Danny goes to his office daily by his car. Depending upon the traffic on the road, he requires petrol as given below :

Monday	240 mL
Tuesday	560 mL
Wednesday	385 mL
Friday	358 mL
Saturday	237 mL

How much petrol would he need on Thursday, if he required 2180 mL of petrol in entire week?

(a) 500 mL (b) 400 mL
(c) 40 mL (d) 600 mL

21. Four bottles contain oil whose volume is shown in the following table. Which two bottles together contain volume less than 4 L 400 mL.

A	3 L 400 mL
B	1 L 650 mL
C	3 L 925 mL
D	2 L 692 mL

(a) *A* and *B* (b) *B* and *C*
(c) *B* and *D* (d) *C* and *A*

22. Four statements are given below. State which of them is true or false and choose the correct option.

I. Very short lengths are measured in millimetre.
II. Long distances are measured in metre.
III. In 1 m, there are 0.001 km.
IV. You can fill 5 glasses of 200 mL from a jug containing 1 L milk.

	I	II	III	IV
(a)	FT	F	T	
(b)	T	F	T	T
(c)	TF	T	F	
(d)	T	T	F	T

Chapter 07

Money

1. $\frac{1}{4}$ of x rupees is equal to 25 paise, then the value of x is

(a) ₹ 1 (b) ₹ 2

(c) ₹ 25 (d) ₹ 3

2. ₹ $7.00 = x \times 50$ paise, then the value of x is

(a) 10 (b) 14

(c) 20 (d) 24

3. Which of the following has the least value?

(a) 280 paise

(b) ₹ 4.85

(c) (5×25) paise

(d) Twenty 10 paise coins

4. Match the following and mark the correct option.

List-I	List-II
I. ₹ 48 ÷ ₹ 3	(i) ₹ 4
II. (16×25) paise	(ii) ₹ 16
III. ₹ 23.25 − ₹ 6.95	(iii) ₹ 19.40
IV. ₹ 19.65 − 25 paise	(iv) ₹ 16.30

	I	II	III	IV
(a)	(ii)	(iii)	(iv)	(i)
(b)	(ii)	(ii)	(i)	(iv)
(c)	(iii)	(iv)	(ii)	(i)
(d)	(ii)	(i)	(iv)	(iii)

5. Compare by using <, > or =.

I. 560 paise ☐ ₹ 7.80.

II. $\frac{2}{3}$ of ₹ 9 ☐ 600 paise.

III. 7 one rupee note ☐ 10 fifty paise coins.

IV. 6 rupees and 25 paise ☐ 5 rupees and 200 paise.

	I	II	III	IV		I	II	III	IV
(a)	<	>	=	<	(b)	>	=	>	>
(c)	>	<	<	>	(d)	<	=	>	<

6. What is the choice of coins you may use for paying ₹ 9.25?

(a) Four ₹ 2 coins, one ₹ 1 coin and one 25 paise coins

(b) Four ₹ 2 coins, one 50 paise coin and one 25 paise coin

(c) One ₹ 5 coin and twelve 50 paise coins

(d) One ₹ 5 coins, two ₹ 1 coins and six 25 paise coins

7. Study the information given below :

Purse | Pairs of gloves | Bow | Winter cap

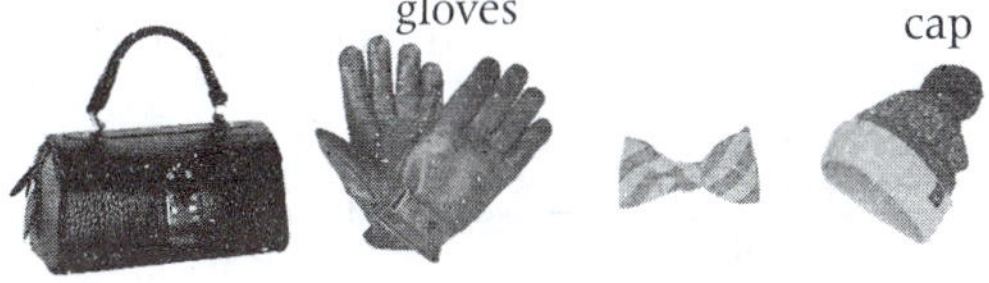

₹ 200 | ₹ 450 | ₹ 50 | ₹ 75

Which of the following statement is correct?

(a) Arti has ₹ 100 by which she can buy a bow and a winter cap.

(b) Alan has ₹ 250 by which he can buy a pair of gloves.

(c) Suzanne is carrying ₹ 500 and she can buy two bows, a winter cap and a purse.

(d) All are correct.

8. State true or false and choose the correct option.

I. Thirty five rupees twenty five paise is equal to ₹ 35.25.

II. ₹ 5.75 means five hundred seventy five rupees.

III. The number of 25 paise coins in ₹ 100 is 40.

IV.

is equal to ₹ 14.85.

	I	II	III	IV		I	II	III	IV
(a)	T	F	F	F	(b)	T	T	F	F
(c)	T	F	F	T	(d)	T	F	T	F

9. Fill in the blanks and choose the correct option.

(i) 30	(ii) 300
(iii) 5	(iv) 50
(v) 10	(vi) 250
(vii) 280	(viii) 75

I. 500 paise makes ₹....... .

II. .... paise makes two and a half rupee.

III. $\frac{3}{4}$ of ₹ 1 = ... paise.

IV. If the cost of 1 cup of tea is ₹ 6, then cost of 5 cups of tea is ₹ ....

	I	II	III	IV		I	II	III	IV
(a)	(v)	(vii)	(iii)	(ii)	(b)	(iii)	(vi)	(i)	(viii)
(c)	(vi)	(i)	(iii)	(iv)	(d)	(iii)	(vi)	(viii)	(i)

10. Jack lives in Dehradun, UK. His uncle lives in Haridwar, UK. On his birthday, Jack received ₹ 200 from his uncle. How many Pencil box can he buy with his birthday money.

If 1 Pencil box =₹40?

(a) 4 (b) 5 (c) 6 (d) 3

11. Christina earns ₹ 100 for every hour as a tuition fees. Last week she worked for 15 hours. She spent 1/4 th of the money she earned. How much money is left with her?

(a) ₹ 1000 (b) ₹ 1125

(c) ₹ 1250 (d) ₹ 1025

12. Hannu wants to buy a video game whose price is ₹ 150. He decided to save ₹ 20 in first week, ₹ 40 in second week, ₹ 60 in third week and so on. After how many weeks will he be able to buy the video game?

Number of weeks	Savings	Total
1	₹ 20	₹ 20
2	₹ 40	₹ 60
3	₹ 60	₹ 120
⋮	⋮	⋮

(a) 5 (b) 3 (c) 6 (d) 4

13. Kirti has some notes which consists of ₹ 1, ₹ 10 and ₹ 50 notes. If her savings is ₹ 415 and she has four ₹ 10 notes and twenty five ₹ 1 notes, then how many notes of ₹ 50 she has?

(a) 7 (b) 8 (c) 6 (d) 9

14. A cricket bat costs ₹ 180. If Bunny has ₹ 500 note, then how much money will he get back?

(a) ₹ 400 (b) ₹ 360
(c) ₹ 320 (d) ₹ 340

15. Andy made bouquet of flowers containing 10 flowers each. He sold the bouquet at ₹ 50. If he had total of 600 flowers. How much did he get in all?

(a) ₹ 3000 (b) ₹ 2500
(c) ₹ 4000 (d) ₹ 2000

16. After purchasing 5 pens for ₹ 17.75 each Stella has ₹ 15.95 left. How much money she had at first?

(a) ₹ 88.75 (b) ₹ 109.50
(c) ₹ 104.70 (d) ₹ 95.95

17. Joshie paid a total of ₹ 572 for 4 toy cars and 6 cookies. Each toy car costs ₹ 38 more than a cookie. What is the cost of each cookie?

(a) ₹ 42 (b) ₹ 56
(c) ₹ 38 (d) ₹ 59

18. Tessie, Adira and Tulip wants to clean out junk. Tessie has 15 kg newspaper, Adira has 13 kg plastic whereas Tulip has 2 kg iron and 4 kg brass. They all went to Ragman whose price list is as shown below.

Ragman Price List

Kinds of Junk	Price of 1 kg
1. Newspaper	₹ 6/-
2. Iron	₹ 14/-
3. Brass	₹ 180/-
4. Plastic	₹ 12/-
5. Waste paper	₹ 4.50/-

Which of the following statement is correct?

(a) Ragman pay ₹ 90 to Adira.
(b) Tulip will get ₹ 784 in return for his junk.
(c) Amount received by Tessie and Adira is more than the amount received by Tulip.
(d) Total money which Ragman had to pay to all the three is ₹ 994.

19.

If the price of one shirt is ₹ 125.75, then how many shirts can I get for ₹ 754.50 with the offer as shown above?

(a) 6 (b) 10
(c) 8 (d) 9

20. Shruti buys 5 notebook worth ₹ 75 each, 2 ruler worth 5.50 each 12 pencils worth ₹ 4 each and one geometry box worth ₹ 82. Choose the correct bill paid by shruti?

(a)

Notebook	–350
Ruler	–11
Pencils	–48
G Box	–81
Total	490

(b)

Notebook	–375
Ruler	–10
Pencils	–49
G Box	–81
Total	515

(c)

Notebook	–375
Ruler	–11
Pencils	–48
G Box	–82
Total	516

(d)

Notebook	–325
Ruler	–12
Pencils	–47
G Box	–82
Total	466

Chapter 08

Time and Calendar

1. Identify the correct time in the clock.

(a) 19 : 50 (b) 17 : 45
(c) 18 : 50 (d) 19 : 40

2. How many minutes should be added to the given time to make it quarter to 5?

(a) 45 min (b) 40 min
(c) 55 min (d) 25 min

3. What will be Greenwich mean time, if Indian standard time is 2 : 55 pm?

Indian Standard Time = Greenwich Mean Time + 5 h 30 min

(a) 10 : 55 pm (b) 9 : 25 pm
(c) 9 : 25 am (d) 9 : 50 am

4. It is 12 : 53 pm in India. What would be the time in USA, if USA is 15 hours ahead of India?

(a) 3 : 52 pm (b) 3 : 53 am
(c) 12 : 43 am (d) 4 : 53 pm

5. On a Sunday morning, it rained from 10 : 07 am till 3 : 15 pm. Calculate the period of rainfall on that Sunday.

(a) 4 h 7 min (b) 5 h 10 min
(c) 5 h 8 min (d) 5 h 7 min

6. If Sunrises at 5 : 52 am on a Wednesday morning and there are 13 hours and 32 minutes of day light, then at what time will the sunset?

(a) 6 : 24 pm (b) 6 : 52 pm
(c) 7 : 24 pm (d) 8 : 54 pm

7. Amelie started baking cake. It took 2 hours and 15 minutes to complete it. She completed it at 17:35.
At what time did she start baking the cake?

(a) 15 : 20 (b) 16 : 35
(c) 15 : 00 (d) 14 : 20

8. State true or false and mark the correct option.

I. 3 h 14 min equals 10814 s.
II. 5 : 30 pm or 16 : 30 are same.
III. 3 h 49 min − 2 h 58 min = 11 min.
IV. 131 hours = 7860 min

	I	II	III	IV		I	II	III	IV
(a)	TT	F	F		(b)	F	F	T	T
(c)	T	F	T	F	(d)	F	F	F	T

9. Match the analog clock with digital clock.

A. 	1. 23 : 55
B. 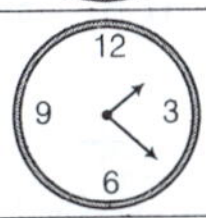	2. 8 : 50
C. 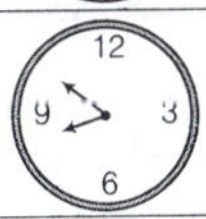	3. 13 : 20
D. 	4. 18 : 30

	A	B	C	D		A	B	C	D
(a)	3	2	1	4	(b)	4	2	3	1
(c)	4	3	2	1	(d)	2	3	4	1

10. Jessica arrived at the nursery at 8 : 12 am on Tuesday morning. How many minutes did she have to wait for the nursery to open?

Market of plants (Nursery)

Days	Open	Close
Monday	9 : 00 am	6 : 00 pm
Tuesday	8 : 30 am	5 : 30 pm
Wednesday	8 : 30 am	6 : 00 pm
Thursday	8 : 00 am	5 : 00 pm
Friday	10 : 00 am	6 : 30 pm

(a) 54 min (b) 30 min
(c) 16 min (d) 18 min

11. A train which was scheduled to come at Shahdra station got 1 h 15 min late. It leaves the station after 10 min and reach Ajmer station at 6 : 00 pm after 8 h of journey.

The train scheduled time to arrive at Shahdra station is

(a) 8 : 35 am (b) 9 : 00 am
(c) 10 : 35 am (d) 10 : 00 am

12. The following table shows the schedule of some flights in 12 h clock format as well as 24 h clock format where some entries are missing writen as P, Q, R, S. Read it and find the missing entries.

Flights	Arrival Time		Departure Time	
	12 h clock time	24 h clock time	12 h clock time	24 h clock time
I	08:30 am	P	Q	14:00
II	R	18:20	2:30 am	S

	P	Q	R	S
(a)	08:30	4:00 pm	8:20 pm	02:30
(b)	08:30	3:00 pm	8:20 pm	01:30
(c)	08:30	2:00 pm	6:20 pm	02:30
(d)	09:30	4:00 pm	7:20 pm	01:30

13. I was flying from London to Sydney with no stop overs. I left London at 2 : 20 pm Tuesday and arrived in Sydney at 6 : 40 pm Wednesday. How long was the flight, if Sydney is 11 h ahead of London?

(a) 17 h (b) 17 h 20 min
(c) 15 h (d) 18 h 40 min

14. If it is Monday on 1st July, then which day of the week will be 15th August?

(a) Thursday (b) Monday
(c) Friday (d) Saturday

15. What is the fraction of the number of days in the month of February in 2012 to the total number of days in that year?

(a) 29/365 (b) 28/365
(c) 29/366 (d) 28/366

16. Julia, Kate, Suzanne and Helena wrote down their birthdays on a slip of paper. Kate and Suzanne have their birthdays in the same month. Julia and Suzanne have their birthdays on the same day but not necessarily in the same month.

June	15th
August	3rd
February	21st
June	21st

Which of the girl was born on August 3rd?

(a) Julia (b) Kate
(c) Suzanne (d) Helena

17. The figure shows the manufacturing and expiry dates of a product.

For how much time did the product last?

(a) 2 yr
(b) 1 yr and 2 months
(c) 1 yr
(d) 2 yr and 1 month

18. Sally got her new phone 1 week and 5 days before from today. If she got the phone on January 15th. What is the date today?

January						
Sun	Mon	Tue	Wed	Thu	Fri	Sat
		1	2	3	4	5
6	7	8	9	10	11	12
13	14	15	16	17	18	19
20	21	22	23	24	25	26
27	28	29	30	31		

(a) 27th January (b) 22nd January
(c) 28th January (d) 26th January

19. Sara takes the piano lessons every third day. If she marks on the calendar her first lesson in March, then on which of the following day in March, Sara will not have any class?

March						
Mon	Tue	Wed	Thu	Fri	Sat	Sun
			1	2	3	4
5	6	7	8	9	10	11
12	13	14	15	16	17	18
19	20	21	22	23	24	25
26	27	28	29	30	31	

(a) Monday (b) Friday
(c) Tuesday (d) Thursday

20. Somya wants to mark her birthday on the given calendar. She know that her birthday is on tenth day before her brother's birthday which is on fourth Tuesday in September 20XX.

SEPTEMBER 20XX						
Mon	Tue	Wed	Thu	Fri	Sat	Sun
				1	2	3
4	5	6	7	8	9	10
11	12	13	14	15	16	17
18	19	20	21	22	23	24
25	26	27	28	29	30	

On which day is Somya's birthday?

(a) 18th September
(b) 19th September
(c) 20th September
(d) 17th September

Chapter 09

Lines and Angles

1. Which of the following is an example of a line?
   (a) Tip of a pencil
   (b) Equator line
   (c) Flashlight
   (d) Edges of paper

2. Which one of the following has one end points?
   (a) Line (b) Line segment
   (c) Ray (d) Angle

3. Jiya makes a line segment of 20 cm. She places an arrow at its one end.
   It is a :
   (a) Line (b) Line segment
   (c) Angle (d) Ray

4. Sara plotted 4 points on a grid. The four points together forms a _____ .

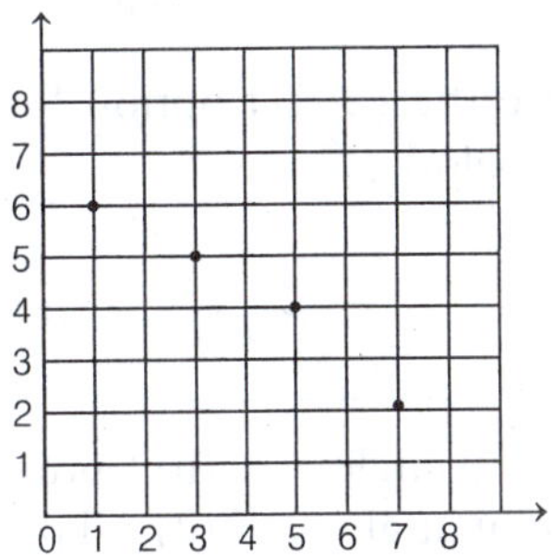

   (a) Straight line
   (b) Square
   (c) Rectangle
   (d) None of the abovee

5. Line *m* and five points are shown on the grid. Which three points appear to lie on the same line that is parallel to line *m*?

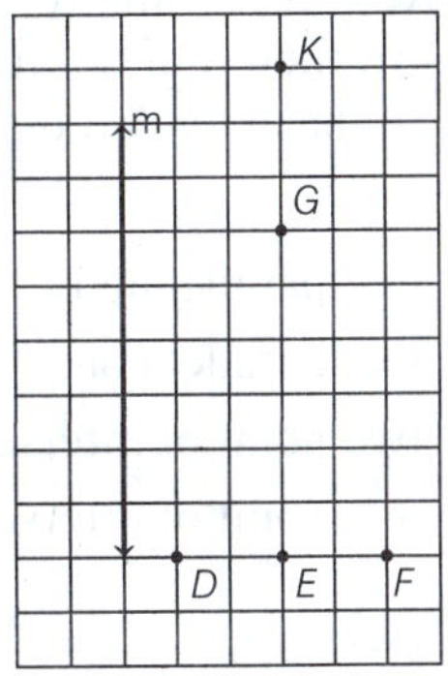

   (a) *K*, *G* and *D* (b) *F*, *D* and *E*
   (c) *K*, *G* and *E* (d) *G*, *F* and *D*

6. Study the given figures. Which of the given figures shows the pair of parallel lines?

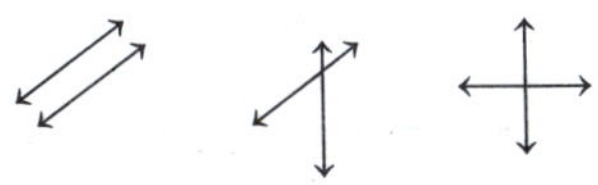

Figure 1 Figure 2 Figure 3

   (a) Figure 1 and 3 (b) Figure 2
   (c) Figure 3 (d) Figure 1

7. Which of the following is an example of intersecting lines?
   (a) Rays from torch
   (b) Railway track
   (c) Adjacent edges of table top
   (d) None of the above

8. Match the following.

(i)	⟷	(A)	Ray
(ii)	——	(B)	Line Segment
(iii)	⟶	(C)	Line

Codes

	(i) (ii) (iii)		(i) (ii) (iii)
(a)	(B), (A), (C)	(b)	(B), (C), (A)
(c)	(A), (B), (C)	(d)	(C), (A), (B)

9. Fill in the blanks.
- A line has P end points.
- A ray has Q end points.
- When two rays or line segments meet at a point, then that point is called R .
- A line can be extended on S sides.

	P	Q	R	S
(a)	one	one	parallel point	all
(b)	two	two	parallel point	both
(c)	one	two	point of intersection	one
(d)	no	one	point of intersection	both

10. How many capital alphabets have curved lines?

(a) 10 (b) 11
(c) 4 (d) 8

11. How many rays are there in the following figure?

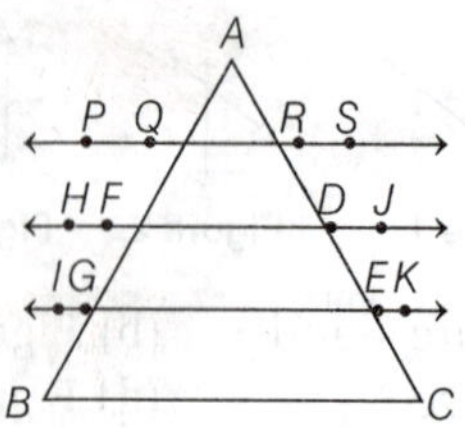

(a) 24 (b) 8
(c) 12 (d) 16

12. In the given figure, if all the points are joined, then how many lines segments will you get?

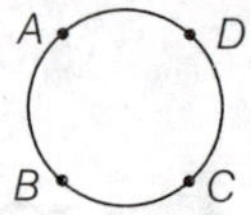

(a) 6 (b) 8
(c) 14 (d) 10

13. How many line segments are there in the given figure?

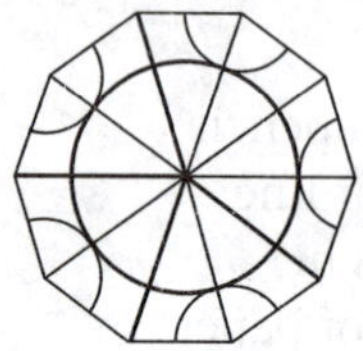

(a) 15 (b) 10
(c) 20 (d) 12

14. How many line segments are there in the following figure?

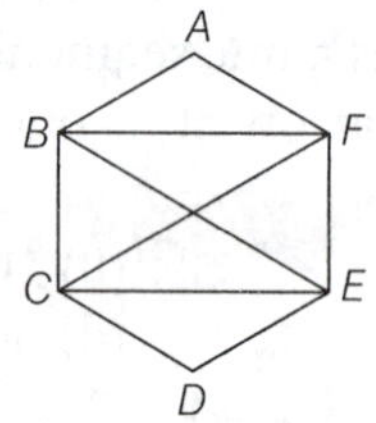

(a) 10 (b) 4
(c) 6 (d) 8

15. Choose the correct option for the angle given below :

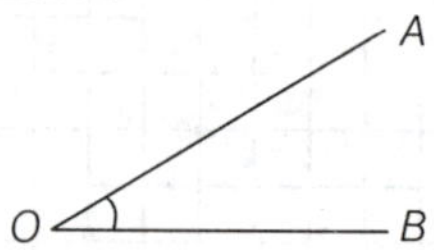

(a) Acute angle (b) Obtuse angle
(c) Right angle (d) All of these

16. Rob makes an angle which measures 147°. Which one of the following types of angle is this?

(a) Obtuse angle (b) Acute angle
(c) Right angles (d) Straight angle

17. Which of the following angles does the given figure contain?

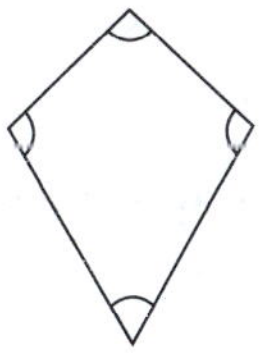

(a) Acute angle (b) Obtuse angle
(c) Right angle (d) All of these

18. Following figure show three clocks showing different times.

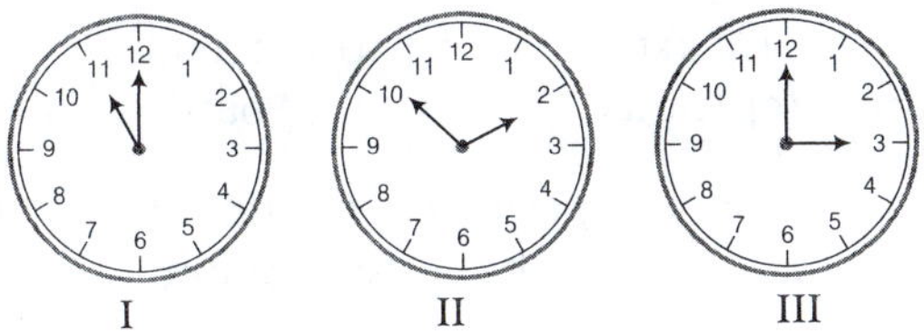

The angle between the hands of the clock is

	I	II	III
(a)	Obtuse	Acute	Right
(b)	Acute	Right	Obtuse
(c)	Acute	Obtuse	Right
(d)	Right	Obtuse	Acute

19. Read the sentence and fill up the blanks with correct option.

A (i) _____. angle measures 90°. An (ii) ___ . angle is less than 90°. A (iii) _____. angle measures equal to two right angles. An obtuse angle is greater than a (iv) ______. angle and less than a straight angle.

(a) (i) Right (ii) Acute (iii) Straight (iv) Right
(b) (i) Obtuse (ii) Obtuse (iii) Acute (iv) 90°
(c) (i) Acute (ii) Straight (iii) Acute (iv) Right
(d) (i) Obtuse (ii) Straight (iii) Acute (iv) Obtuse

20. How many angles are there in the figure?

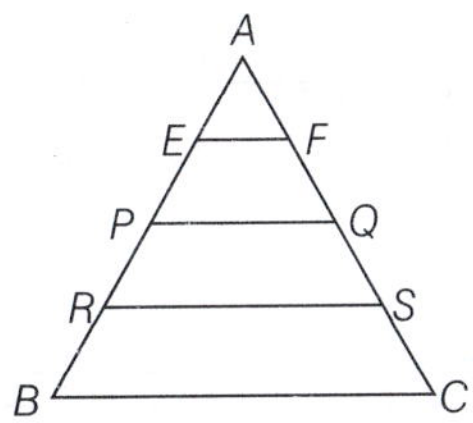

(a) 7 (b) 15
(c) 9 (d) 4

Chapter 10

Area and Perimeter

1. What is the perimeter of the given triangle?

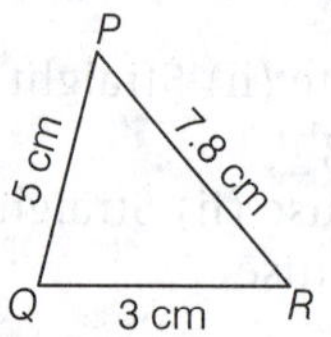

(a) 14.2 cm (b) 16.8 cm
(c) 15.8 cm (d) 16.2 cm

2.

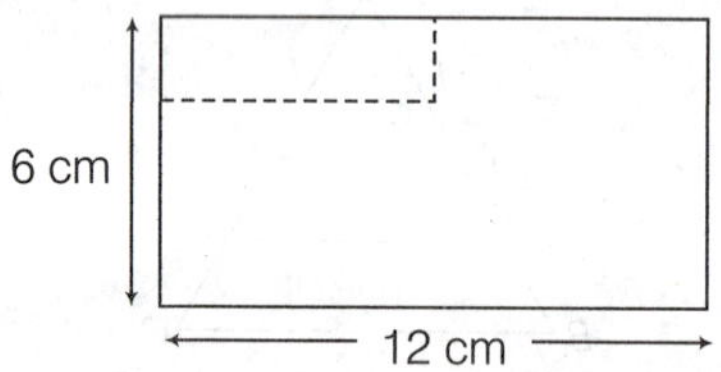

Cyra is given a homework to cut-out a piece of rectangle out of a given sheet. If the breadth of the cut-out figure is 1/3rd of the breadth of the sheet as shown in the diagram, then the perimeter of the cut-out figure will be

(a) 12 m (b) 24 m
(c) 16 m (d) 36 m

Directions (Q. Nos. 3 and 4) The given table shows the dimension of gardens in an apartment.

Garden	**Length** (in m)	**Breadth** (in m)
A	12	8
B	14	12
C	10	8
D	14	5

3. Which garden has the largest boundary?
(a) *A* (b) *B* (c) *C* (d) *D*

4. If the breadth of the smallest garden is increased by 4 m, then what will be the position of that garden, if we arrange them in ascending order on the basis of perimeter?
(a) First (b) Second
(c) Third (d) Fourth

5. Find the perimeter of the given figure and choose the correct option.

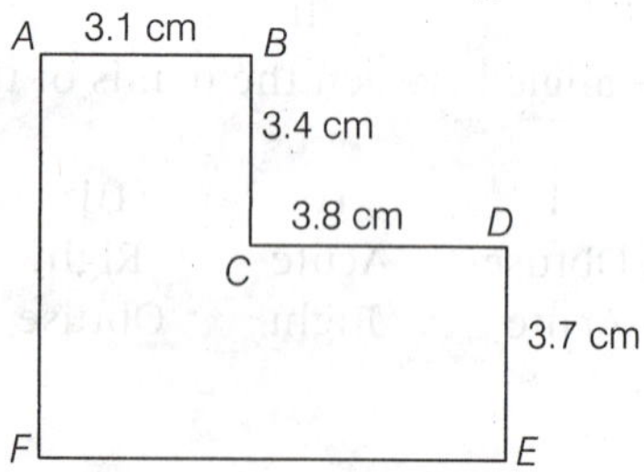

(a) 28 cm (b) 30 cm
(c) 25 cm (d) 42 cm

6. The perimeter of the figure 1 (All sides are equal) is same as the perimeter of the figure 2 (All sides are equal). If each side of figure 1 is 8 cm long, then each side of figure 2 is _____.

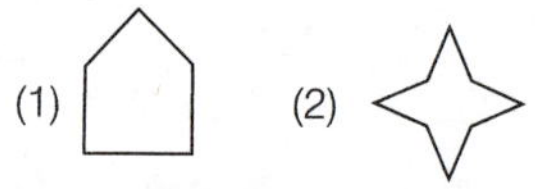

(a) 8 cm (b) 6 cm
(c) 5 cm (d) 10 cm

7. Ishika jogged around a field of a given shape 5 times. How far did the Ishika jogged?

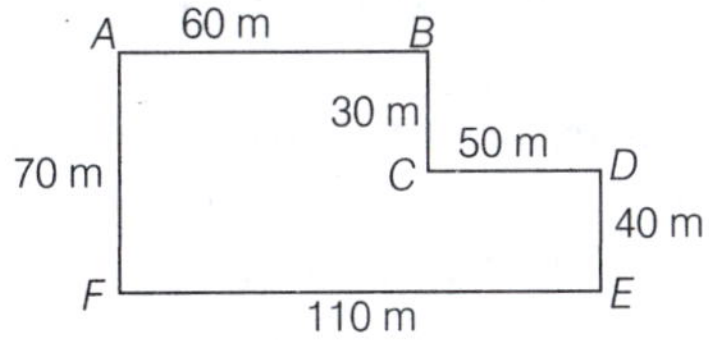

(a) 1600 m
(b) 1800 m
(c) 1200 m
(d) 2000 m

8. Figures (i) and (ii) show two identical rectangles A and B which are arranged differently. What is the difference in the perimeter of the figures (i) and (ii)?

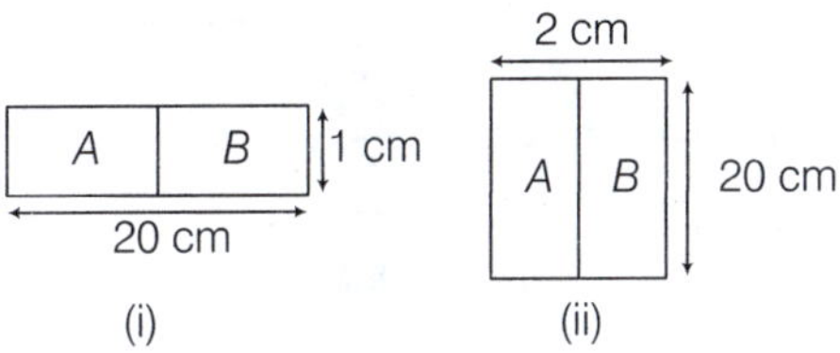

(a) 2 cm
(b) 4 cm
(c) 6 cm
(d) Both have same perimeter

9.

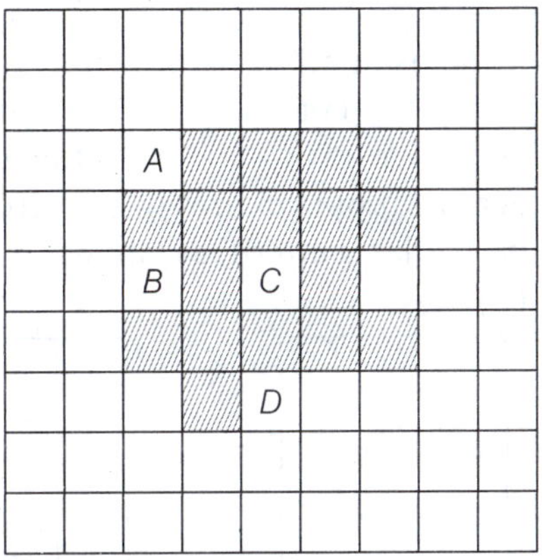

Celestia had some squares of area 1 sq. unit by which she made the above figure. She is left with 1 square. Where should the square be placed, so that the perimeter of the given figure gets reduced by 4 units?

(a) At A (b) At B
(c) At C (d) At D

10. The cow is grazing in a field given below. Then, the area in which the cow can graze is

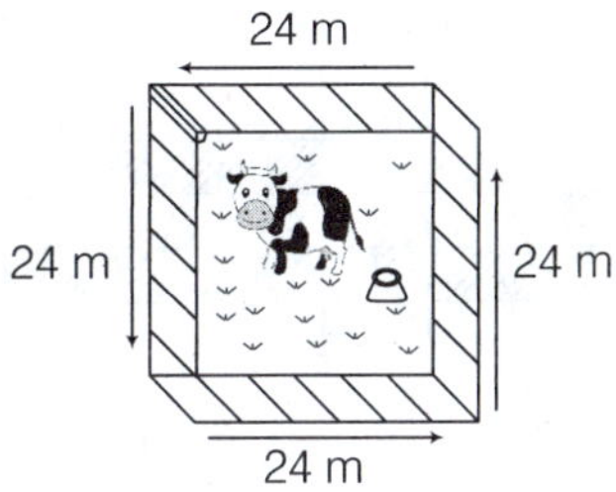

(a) 576 m^2 (b) 286 m^2
(c) 48 m^2 (d) 76 m^2

11. Gregor has a piece of bread. He divided it into four pieces. If dimension of the bread is given, then the area of each piece is

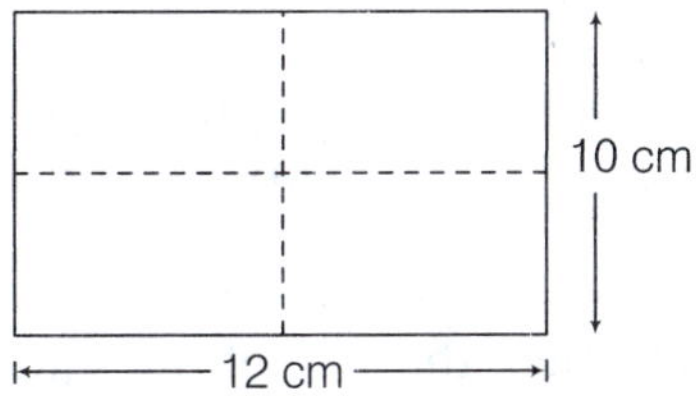

(a) 11 cm^2 (b) 120 cm^2
(c) 30 cm^2 (d) 22 cm^2

12. If each square has area 1 sq. unit, then the area of the given figure is

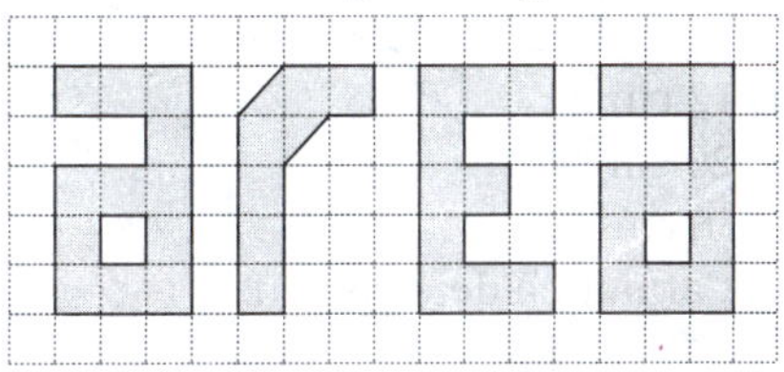

(a) 30 sq. units
(b) 40 sq. units
(c) 42 sq. units
(d) 41 sq. units

Directions (Q. Nos. 13-14) Study the following information and answer the questions.

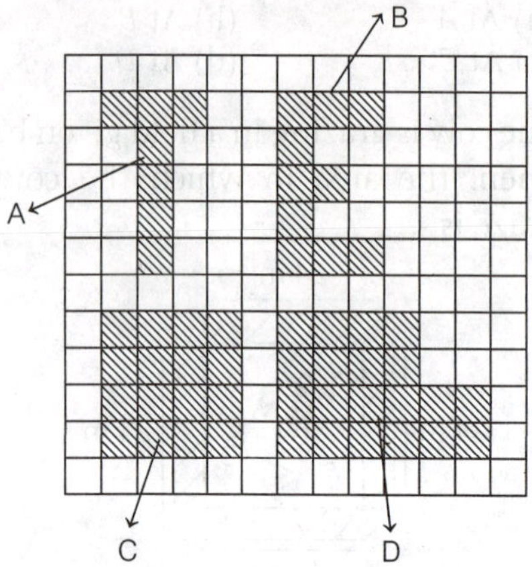

13. If each square has area 1 cm^2, then which following given shapes occupies smallest area?

(a) A (b) B
(c) C (d) D

14. Which of the two given shapes have a total area of 26 sq. units?

(a) A and B (b) B and D
(c) B and C (d) A and C

15. A circle is inscribed in a square as shown below. Then, the area of the square is

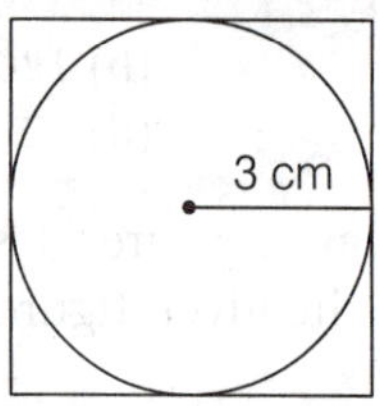

(a) 12 cm^2
(b) 20 cm^2
(c) 36 cm^2
(d) Cannot be determined

16. Area of Frank's backyard is 20 sq. ft and he wants the basketball court of length 5 ft and breadth 4 ft to be placed into his backyard. Does Frank have enough space?

(a) Yes, the backyard is big enough because both the backyard and basketball court are equal.
(b) No, because basketball court is 24 sq. ft
(c) Yes, because backyard has more area than basketball court.
(d) Cannot be determined

17. Some girls play in a park whose dimensions are given. One day, two of them had a fight with the rest of the girls and then they decided to separate the area where they can play. They shared the area of park equally among them. How much area will be occupied by the remaining girls?

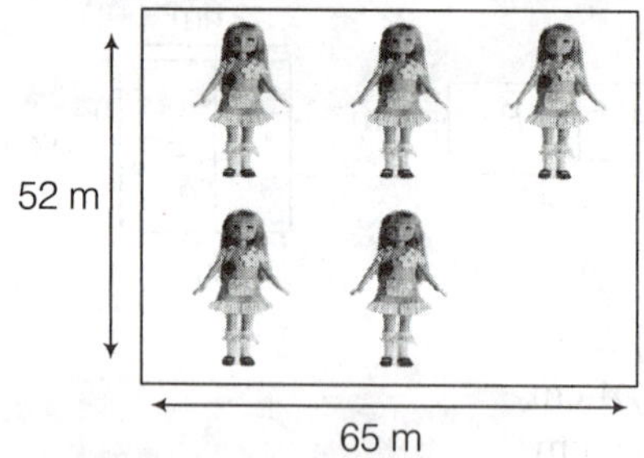

(a) 1685 m^2 (b) 2704 m^2
(c) 1352 m^2 (d) 2028 m^2

18. Alina is making a design using craft paper. She cut out a square of side 40 cm as shown in figure (A). After that she again cut out squares of side 10 cm in a particular pattern as shown in figure (B).

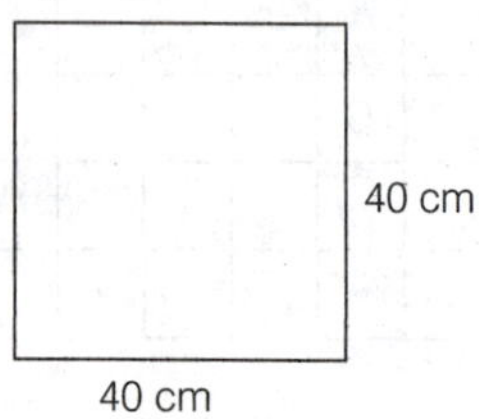

Figure (A)

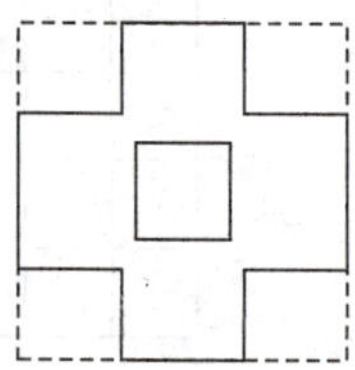

Figure (B)

Look at the figures carefully and calculate the difference between the area of figure (A) and figure (B)?

(a) 500 cm^2 (b) 1600 cm^2
(c) 1100 cm^2 (d) 1500 cm^2

19. Miss Michelle decided to paint a wall of her house whose length is 28 m and breadth is 21 m. If she painted one-third of the wall green and half of the remaining wall blue, then how much portion she still needs to paint?

(a) 98 m^2 (b) 392 m^2
(c) 294 m^2 (d) 196 m^2

20. The perimeters of two squares are 40 cm and 32 cm. If the perimeter of the third square is equal to the difference of the perimeters of first two squares, then what will be the side of the third square

(a) 2 cm (b) 4 cm
(c) 64 cm (d) 8 cm

21. A garden is in the shape of rectangle having a path in it as shown in figure below. Find the area of garden excluding the walking path.

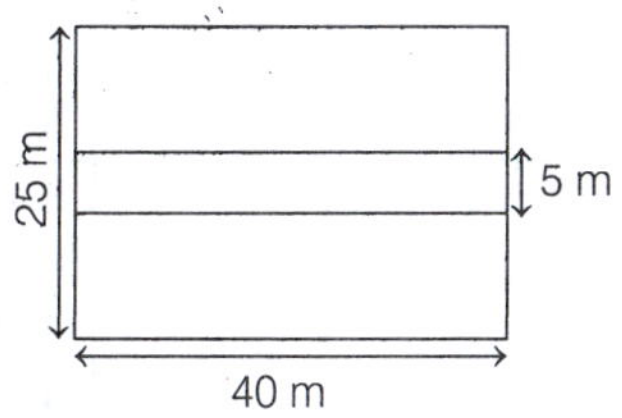

(a) 750 m^2 (b) 800 m^2
(c) 900 m^2 (d) 1000 m^2

22. Rahul and Rosy took part in a race. The racing track is circular in shape. Rahul runs faster than Rosy, yet he loses the race. The reason for this is

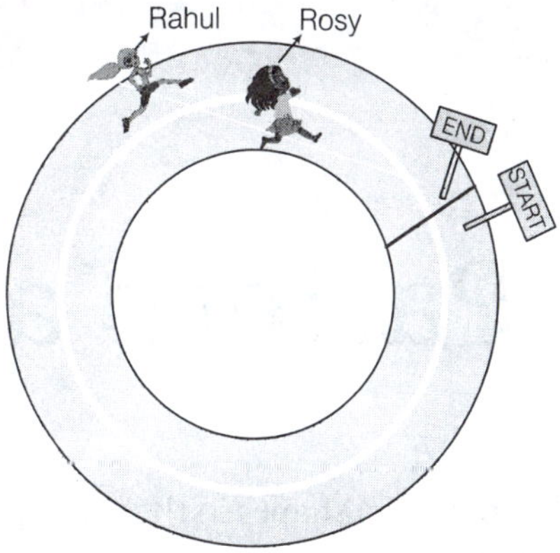

(a) The perimeter of inner circle is less than the perimeter of outer circle.
(b) The area of inner circle is less than the area of outer circle.
(c) Both have different start.
(d) Cannot be determined

23. Fill in the blanks and choose the correct option.

(i) Area	(ii) 2 *abc*
(iii) 5 × sides	(iv) a + b + c
(v) 15	(vi) Perimeter
(vii) 30	(viii) 6 × sides

I. __ is expressed in the units of length.
II. Perimeter of a triangle with sides a, b and c is _____ .
III. Perimeter of a regular hexagon is _____ .
IV. Area of 15 unit squares is ____ square units.

	I	II	III	IV
(a)	(vi)	(iii)	(viii)	(vii)
(b)	(i)	(ii)	(iii)	(v)
(c)	(vi)	(iv)	(viii)	(v)
(d)	(i)	(viii)	(iii)	(vii)

Chapter 11

Pattern and Symmetry

1. The next two shapes in the given pattern will be

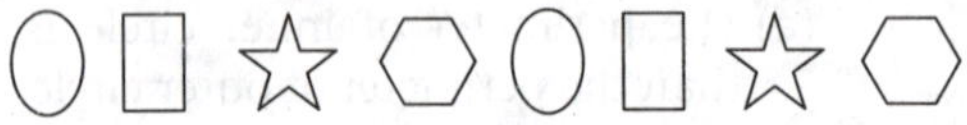

(a)  (b) 

(c)  (d) 

2. Cyra is playing. She is showing her friends that she can stand on her head. If she continue this play, i.e., stands up and then upside down. What will be her position in 13th turn?

(a)  (b) 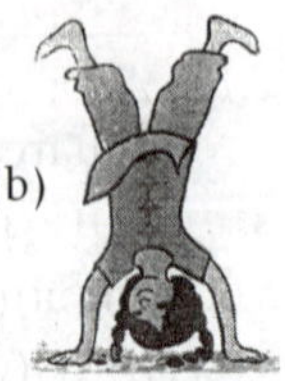

(c)  (d) Cannot be determined

3. 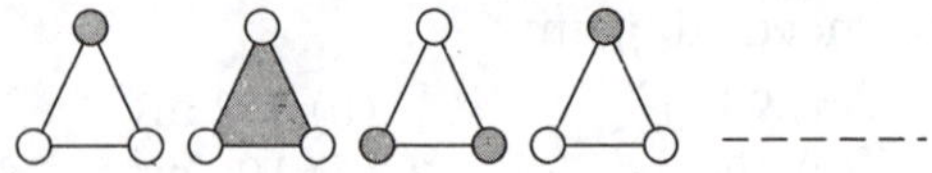

If the above pattern continues in the same way, till 20th term, then how many times  will occur in the pattern?

(a) 4 (b) 6
(c) 7 (d) 3

4. Find the next term in the given pattern.

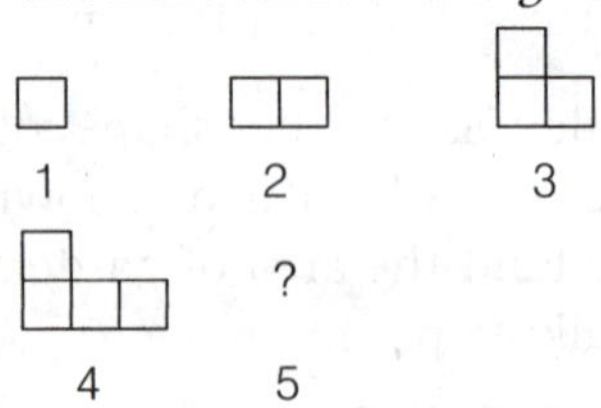

(a) 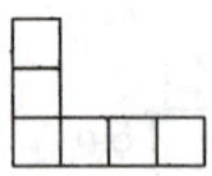 (b) 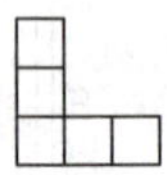

(c) 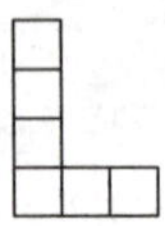 (d) 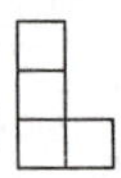

5. Find the next figure in the given pattern.

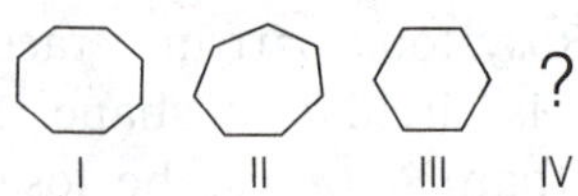

(a) 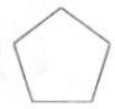 (b) 

(c)  (d) 

Directions (Q. Nos. 6 and 7) Each question follows a certain pattern. Identify the pattern and choose the odd one out.

6. (a) 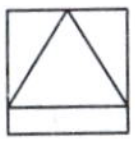 (b) 

(c) 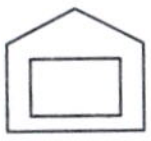 (d) 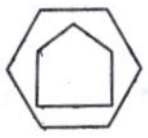

7. (a) 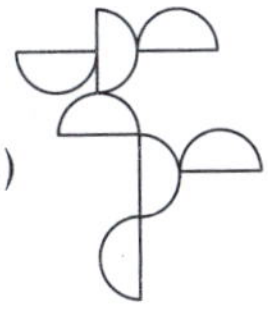 (b) 

(c)  (d) 

8. Study the pattern and find the missing term.

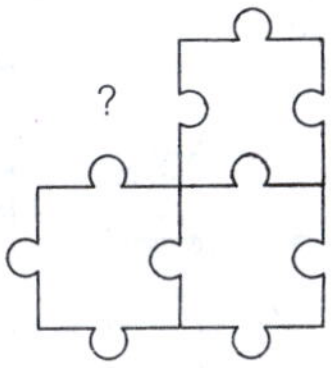

(a)  (b) 

(c)  (d) 

9. The first 8 shapes of a pattern are shown below :

What will be the next shape?

(a)  (b)  (c)  (d) 

10. Replace the question mark (?) with the correct image.

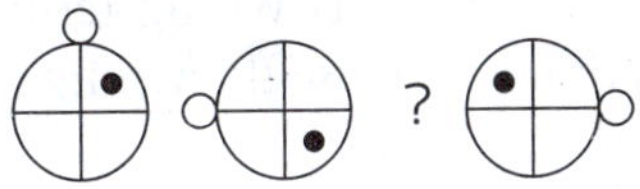

(a) 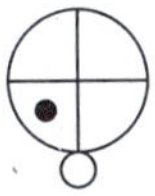 (b) 

(c)  (d) 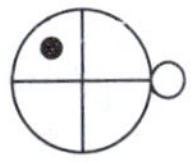

11. Observe the pattern in Ist and IIIrd row and use it to find the value of *A*.

9	4	36
5	*A*	60
12	7	84

(a) 12 (b) 6
(c) 11 (d) 10

12. Identify the pattern and find the difference between *A* and *B*.

(39) (52) (65) (*A*) (91) (*B*)

(a) 26 (b) 40
(c) 58 (d) 78

13. Identify the pattern in the sequence

0, 1, 1, 2, 3, 5, 8, 13, ...

(a) Add 1 to the previous term to get the next term.

(b) Add 2 to the previous term to get the next term.

(c) Add the previous terms to get the next term.

(d) Multiply the previous terms to get the next term.

14. Kanchi has made a pattern of numbers as shown below. She wants to check whether there is any wrong term in the pattern or not. Choose the wrong number in pattern.

$10000 - 800 = 9200$
$9200 - 800 = 8400$
$8400 - 800 = 7600$

(a) 10000 (b) 7600

(c) 8400 (d) All are correct

15. Which one of the following is a symmetric figure?

(a) 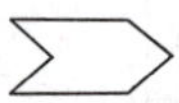 (b) 

(c)  (d) 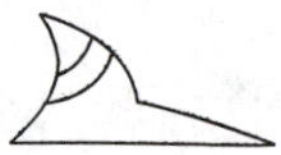

16. Which one of the following figures has no line of symmetry?

(a)  (b) 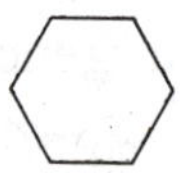

(c)  (d) 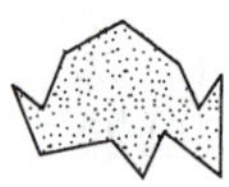

17. Which of the following letters has exactly one line of symmetry?

(a) D (b) H (c) O (d) X

18. Which of the following alphabets is symmetrical along vertical line of symmetry?

(a) A (b) Q (c) K (d) Z

19. Find the number of lines of symmetry of the following figure.

(a) 0 (b) 1 (c) 3 (d) 2

20. What is the minimum number of square that must be shaded so that the line OP becomes a line of symmetry?

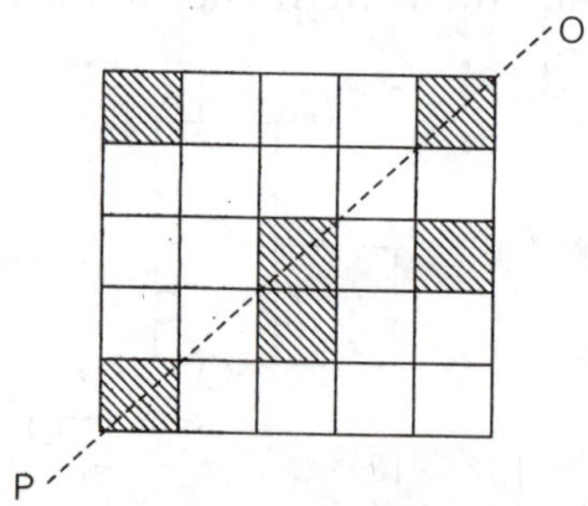

(a) 3 (b) 2 (c) 4 (d) 1

Chapter

12

Data Handling

1. The pictograph shows how much a family spends on different things every month.

Rent	□ □
Food	□ □ □ □
Transport	□
Others	□ □ □

Here, □ = ₹ 1000

What does the family spend the most on?

(a) Rent (b) Food

(c) Transport (d) Others

2. The following pictograph shows number of students present in the class in different days of a week. Find the total number of students present on Thursday.

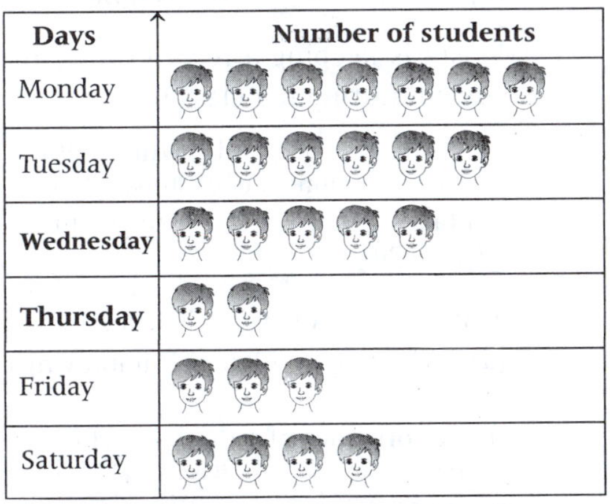

Here, one (face) represent 10 students.

(a) 20 (b) 30 (c) 40 (d) 50

3. The pictograph shows number of trees planted in different cities in year 2019.

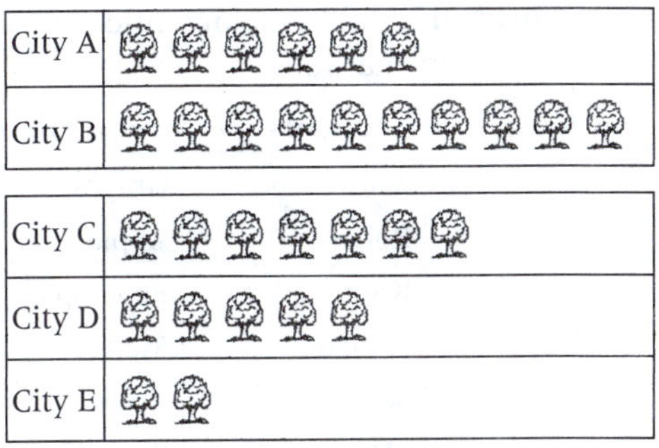

Here one (tree) represent 500 trees.

Which city planted most number of trees?

(a) A (b) B

(c) C (d) E

Directions (Q. Nos. 4 and 5) The following pictograph shows the number of ice-creams sold within 4 days in an ice-cream parlour. Study it and answer the questions.

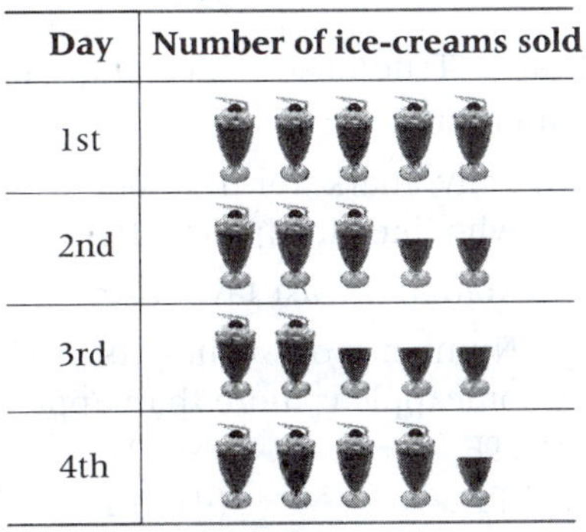

Given,  = 4 ice-creams

and  = 2 ice-creams

4. On which day, 14 ice-creams were sold?

(a) 1st (b) 2nd (c) 3rd (d) 4th

5. On which two days, a total of 36 ice-creams were sold?

(a) 2 and 4 (b) 1 and 3
(c) 3 and 4 (d) 1 and 2

Directions (Q.Nos. 6 and 7) Class teacher, Mr. Anil was creating a chart of fruits. He had to decide what are the favourite fruit of students. The students choose the following.

Read the table below and answer the question that follow :

S. No.	Students	Fruit choice
1.	Sally	Grapes
2.	Rohan	Apple
3.	Kiran	Pineapple
4.	Deepak	Mango
5.	Sara	Apple
6.	Mohan	Pineapple
7.	Sunita	Apple
8.	Arun	Pineapple
9.	Zeenut	Mango
10.	Jay	Pineapple

6. How many students like apples?

(a) III (b) 𝍸
(c) IIII (d) 𝍸 I

7. State True/false for the following statements.

A. Tally mark for number of students who like pineapple is IIII.

B. Mango is least favourite.

C. Number of students who like pineapple is more than apple.

(a) TTF (b) FTF
(c) TFF (d) TFT

8. Natasha has done a survey to show how many rainy days in her town during the first half of the year.

S. No.	Months	Tally Marks
1.	January	𝍸
2.	February	II
3.	March	IIII
4.	April	𝍸 II
5.	May	𝍸 𝍸 III
6.	June	𝍸 𝍸 𝍸

Which month has the most rainy day?

(a) April (b) June
(c) January (d) May

9. A school had organised a quiz competition in which there were four teams who took part. A total of 10 questions were asked from them.

The following table shows the number of points scored by each team.

Teams	Red	Blue	Green	Yellow
Points	7	9	10	8

Which team scored second position in the quiz competition?

(a) Red (b) Blue
(c) Green (d) Yellow

10. Krista is keeping a record of the marks she got during her class tests.

Date	1st June	3rd June	7th June	12th June	17th June
Marks (Out of 20)	15	14	10	19	13

Which of the following is true?

(a) Performance of Krista is improving each day.

(b) Performance of Krista is declining each day.

(c) Performance of Krista cannot be determined.

(d) None of the above

11. Eliana is very fond of collecting data. She made the following list of those houses in her colony who have a particular pet.

Pet	Dog	Cat	Rabbit	Tortoise	Parrot	
Frequency	12	7	☐	1	5	30

How many houses have rabbit as their pet?

(a) 4 (b) 8 (c) 5 (d) 6

12. The given chart shows the number of children of class IV which have their birthdays in the given three months.

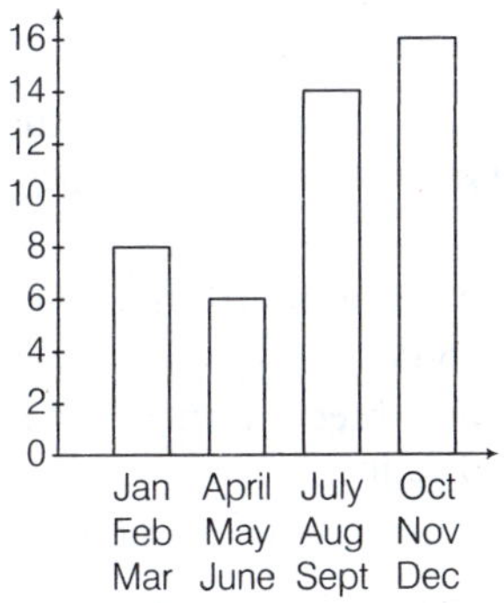

If no children have birthday in July and only 4 children have birthday in August, then how many children have their birthdays in September?

(a) 14 (b) 12 (c) 10 (d) 16

13. The following bar graph shows the sale of books of a store in four different months. Then, the total sale of books in four months is

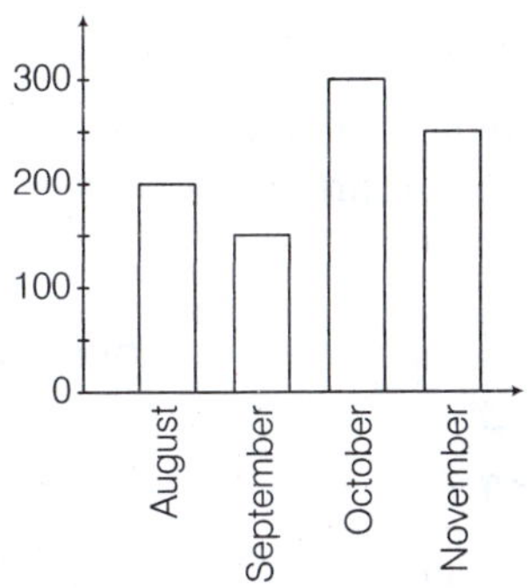

(a) 750 (b) 1000
(c) 900 (d) 850

Directions (Q. Nos. 14 and 15) Venkateshwara Global school conducted a survey of class IV to identify the interest of students in different Olympiads. The data is as follows :

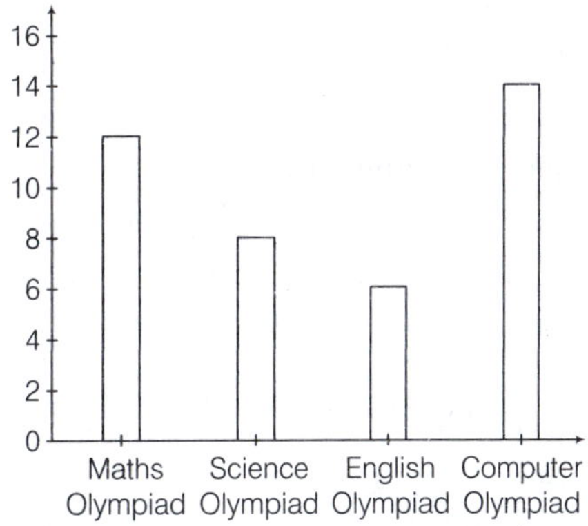

14. In which Olympiad, students are interested the most?

(a) Maths (b) Science
(c) English (d) Computer

15. How many more students are interested in Maths Olympiad than English Olympiad?

(a) 14 (b) 8 (c) 6 (d) 10

Directions (Q. Nos. 16-18) Consider the following bar graph and answer the questions.

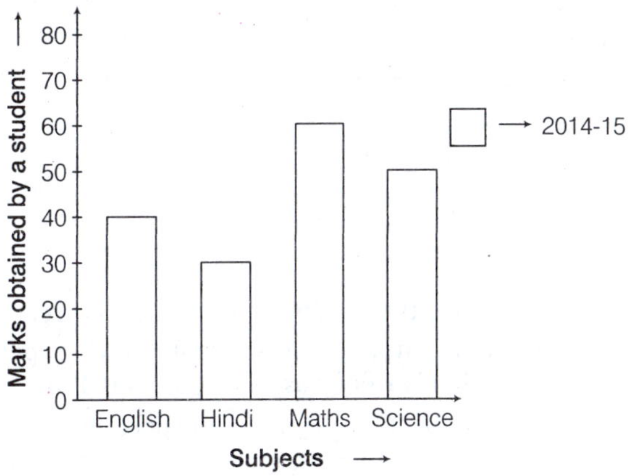

16. What is the information given by the bar graph?
(a) Marks obtained by a student in four subjects.
(b) Marks obtained by a student in session 2014-15.
(c) Marks obtained by a student in three subjects.
(d) Both (a) and (b)

17. In which subject did the student score second highest marks?
(a) English (b) Hindi
(c) Maths (d) Science

18. In which subject did the student's score is $\frac{3}{4}$th of the score in English?
(a) Maths (b) Hindi
(c) Science (d) None of these

19. Consider the given bar graph showing the number of students who have pet animals in the different classes and answer the following question.

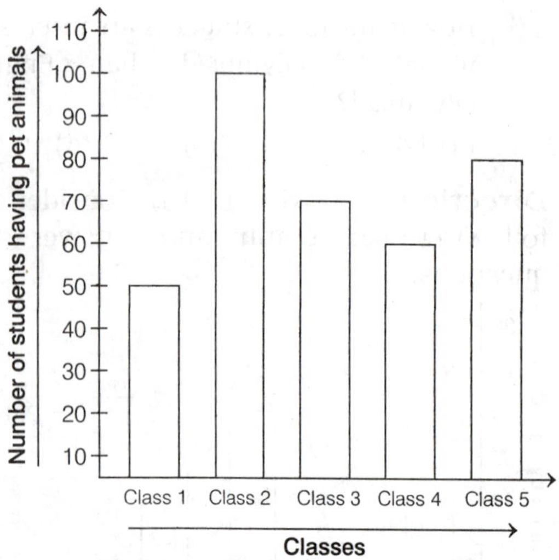

Which of the following options is correct?
(a) Total number of students having pet animals from class 1 to class 5 is 110.
(b) Number of students having pet animals in class 2 is 40 more than that to class 4.
(c) The fraction of students having pet animals in class 3 to that of class 5 is $\frac{3}{8}$.
(d) None of the above

20. The D' lites fast food shop wants to find out the likings of their customers whether they like burger, fries or cold coffee. They come up with the following chart.

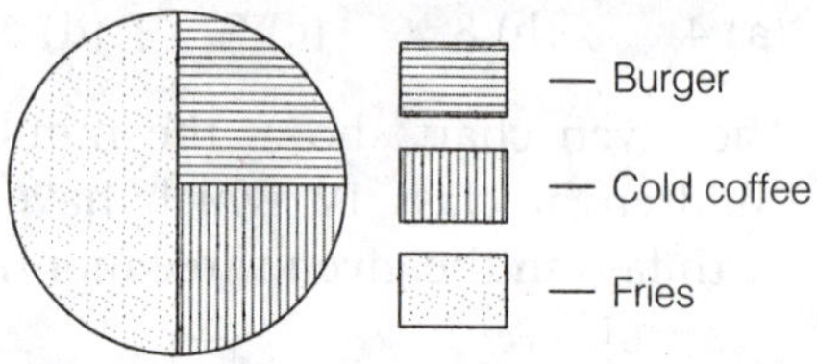

Which of the following is true?
(a) About one-fourth of the customers like fries.
(b) About one-fourth of the customers like burgers.
(c) About three-fourth of the customers like cold coffees.
(d) No customer likes burgers.

21. Class IV consists of 28 children. All children of the class are getting ready for a drama. Some children are acting, some are busy in collecting dresses while some are bringing chairs and tables to make the sets.

Work	Number of children
Acting	14
Collecting dresses	7
Making sets	7

Which of the following pie chart would be most appropriate to depict the above information?

(a)  (b) 

(c)  (d) 

PRACTICE SET 01

1. When 78456 is multiplied by P, we get 2589048. Find the value of P.

(a) 32 (b) 40
(c) 33 (d) 35

2. Find the product of the face and place value of 3's in the number 27345.

(a) 900 (b) 3000
(c) 9000 (d) 90

3. Study the figure given below.

What fraction of the above figure is shaded?

(a) $\frac{12}{12}$ (b) $\frac{6}{12}$
(c) $\frac{8}{12}$ (d) $\frac{9}{12}$

4. On the basis of following features identify the correct name.

A. It is denoted by $\angle$
B. It is measured in degrees.
C. It is the gap between the 2 rays.

(a) Ray (b) Line
(c) Point (d) Angle

5. In the given letter what type of line of symmetry?

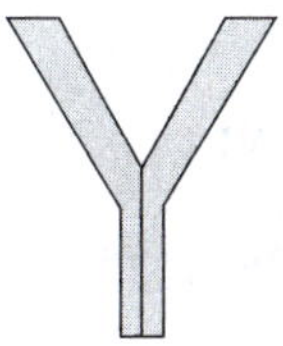

(a) Horizontal
(b) Vertical
(c) No line of symmetry
(d) Diagonal

6. Find the value of x.

(a) 1 (b) 3
(c) 4 (d) 5

7. If each square has area $1\ cm^2$, then which of the following given shapes occupies largest area?

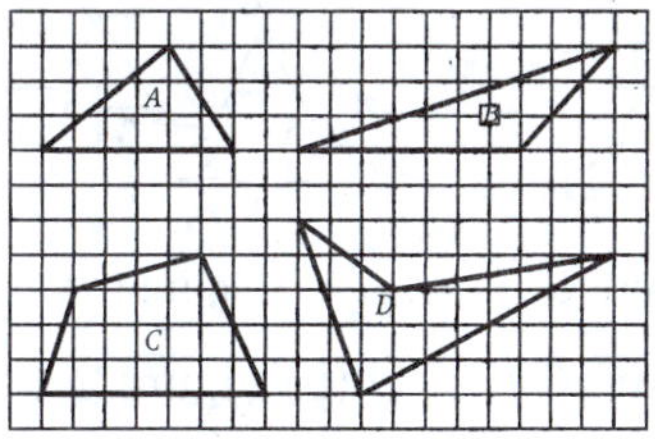

(a) A (b) B
(c) C (d) D

8. A traffic light changes its colour after every 2 minutes in the order as follows :

red → yellow → green

If it is red now and time is 5 : 20 pm, then at what time light becomes green, if it stopped working for 25 minutes?

(a) 5 : 40 pm (b) 5 : 50 pm
(c) 5 : 49 pm (d) 5 : 47 pm

9. What is the weight of box Q?

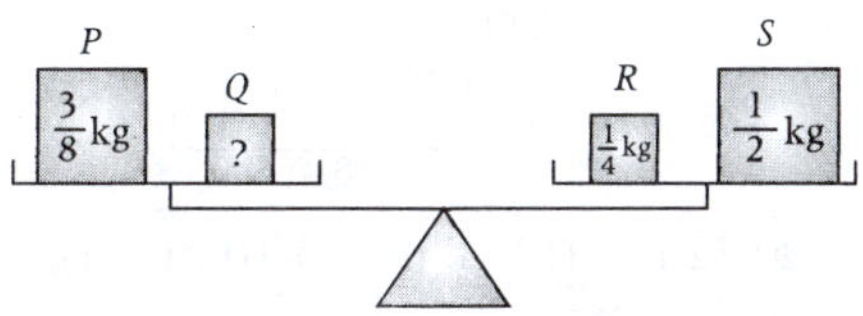

(a) $\frac{2}{3}$ kg (b) $\frac{3}{8}$ kg

(c) $\frac{1}{6}$ kg (d) $\frac{3}{2}$ kg

10. Which figure shows the correct factor tree of 24?

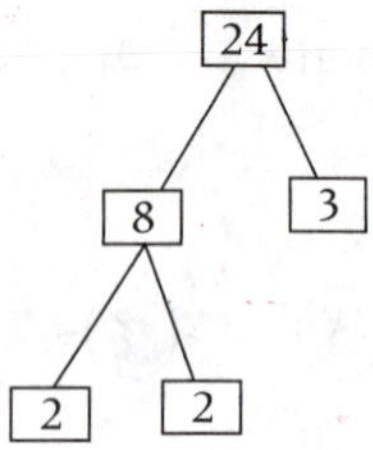

Figure A

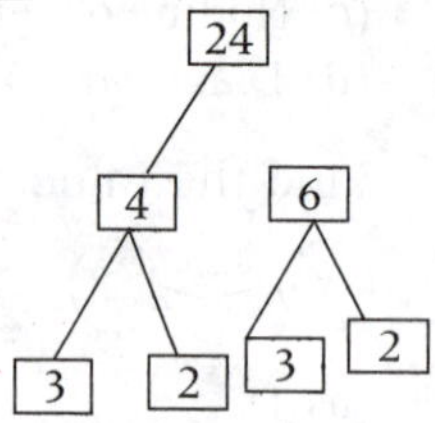

Figure B

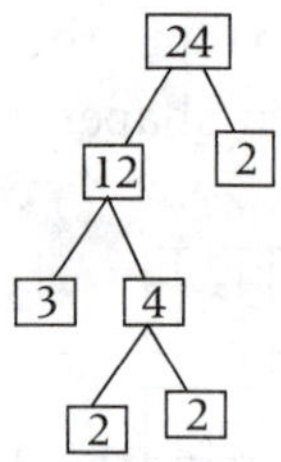

Figure C

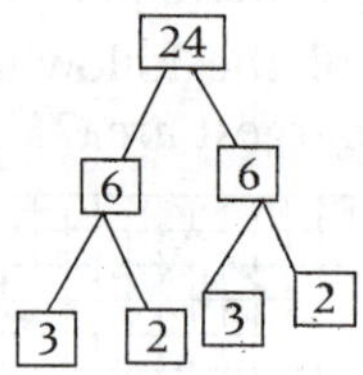

Figure D

(a) Figure C (b) Figure D
(c) Figure B (d) Figure A

11. Avinash hired a taxi. It charges ₹ 8 for the first kilometre and ₹ 10 for the successive kilometres. How much money Avinash had to pay, if he travelled 58 km?

(a) ₹ 472 (b) ₹ 590
(c) ₹ 500 (d) ₹ 588

12. An ant is crawling from point *A* to point *B* using the staircase. How many metre distance will it crawl to reach point *B*?

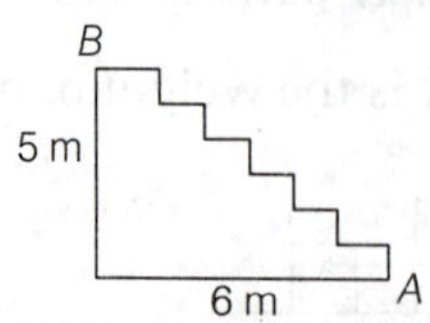

(a) 12 m (b) 30 m (c) 10 m (d) 11 m

13. Match the following and choose the correct option.

A.	Greatest 3-digit number + 1	1.	1185 lakh
B.	12 crore − 15 lakh	2.	CCLXXVII
C.	135 hundred + 5 hundred	3.	M
D.	CXXXV + CXLII	4.	14 thousand

Codes

	A	B	C	D
(a)	3	4	1	2
(b)	1	3	2	4
(c)	3	1	4	2
(d)	2	3	4	1

14. A cricket stadium has 428 rows with 190 seats in each row. How many seats are there in the stadium?

(a) 81320
(b) 83210
(c) 91320
(d) 93000

15. The cost of a Book, Hockey stick, Bottle and Paper clip is given.

Items	Costs losts in roman numbers
Book	LXXXVI
Hockey stick	CLV
Bottle	LXVII
Paper clip	XXV

What is the total cost of a paper clip, hockey stick and a book?

(a) CCLXVI
(b) CXV
(c) CCXLVI
(d) CCXLI

16. How many triangles are there in the given figure?

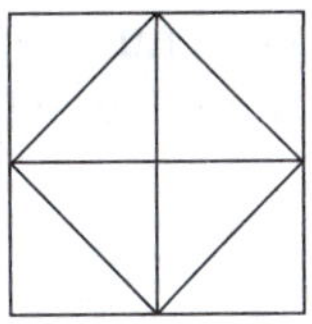

(a) 12 (b) 8
(c) 14 (d) 10

17. The graph shows the number of plants Krista and her friends planted each day in a garden.

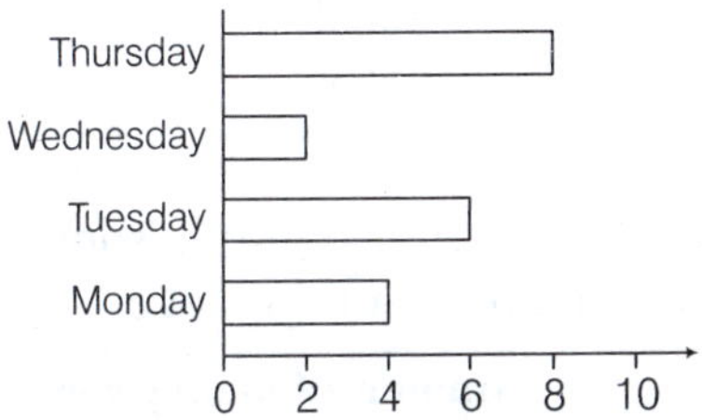

If each sapling requires 30 minutes to get planted and they started planting at 5 : 00 O'clock in the evening on Tuesday, then at what time Krista and her friends get their work done?

(a) 8:00 am (b) 8:00 pm
(c) 7:00 pm (d) 7:30 pm

Directions (Q. Nos. 18 and 19) A college library has the following fine charges for delay in returning of a book.

First day	₹ 1
Second day	₹ 1
Third day	₹ 2
Fourth day	₹ 3
Successive days	₹ 5

If the book is lost or tear, then students have to pay the double price of the book.

18. Kathlean borrowed a book from library and returned it after four days of date of returning.

How much fine does Kathlean has to submit to library?

(a) ₹ 5 (b) ₹ 6
(c) ₹ 7 (d) ₹ 8

19. If Kathlean lost the book, then how much amount will librarian charge, if the cost of book is ₹ 192.65?

(a) ₹ 385.30 (b) ₹ 354.28
(c) ₹ 122.85 (d) ₹ 659.23

20. How many line segments are there in the figure?

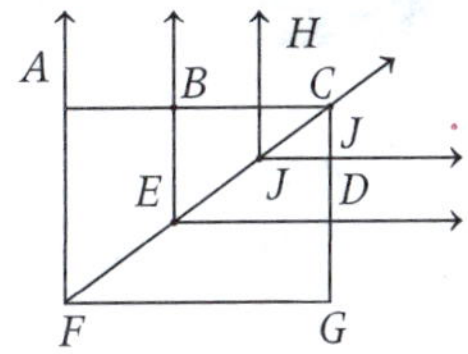

(a) 5 (b) 7
(c) 9 (d) 22

21. Following figure shows the magic pattern in which every row, column and diagonal follow certain pattern. Identify the pattern and complete it.

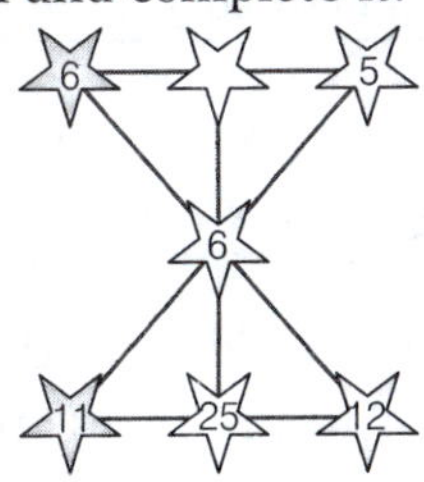

(a) 24 (b) 12
(c) 4 (d) 19

22. Sparsh travelled 18 km in 2 days. On the Ist day, he covered $5\frac{1}{2}$ km. How much distance did he covered on the 2nd day?

(a) $7\frac{1}{2}$ km (b) $15\frac{1}{2}$ km
(c) $12\frac{1}{2}$ km (d) $8\frac{1}{2}$ km

23. Jimmy is playing a racing game. The fraction below each car shows the time taken by the car to finish the race.
With the help of the time given. Identify the position of cars in which they will finish the race.

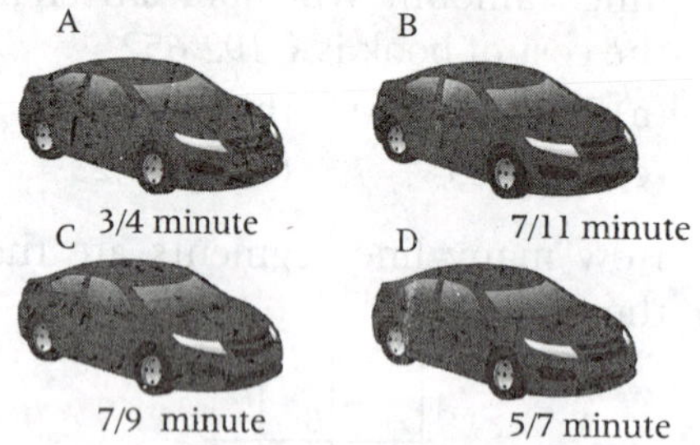

(a) $C < D < A < B$ (b) $B < C < D < A$
(c) $B < D < A < C$ (d) $A < D < B < C$

24. Zane found a page from 2008 calendar. He found a note on the page.
I am going for shopping on the last Saturday of May. Six days later, I am going to UK.
David

May 2008						
Sun	Mon	Tue	Wed	Thu	Fri	Sat
				1	2	3
4	5	6	7	8	9	10
	12	13	14	15	16	17

When did David go to UK?
(a) 30th May, 2008 (b) 5th June, 2008
(c) 1st June, 2008 (d) 6th June, 2008

25. Vishesh earns ₹ 721 in a week. How much money does he earn in 16 days?
(a) ₹ 1648 (b) ₹ 1500
(c) ₹ 1240 (d) ₹ 1200

26. Amisha is driving at a speed of 60 km/h covering 320 km. How much distance did Amisha cover when rounding off to nearest hundred?
(a) 300 (b) 350
(c) 330 (d) 325

27. The given chart shows the number of pencils students have. Which two students have number of pencils that could be shared equally among three students?

Students	Number of pencils
Prashant	13
Radhika	12
Sonal	19
Neha	15

(a) Prashant and Radhika
(b) Radhika and Sonal
(c) Radhika and Neha
(d) Sonal and Neha

28. The incomplete pictograph shows the amount of money Anuj spent on 4 days.

Day	Amount of money spent
Wednesday	₹ ₹ ₹ ₹
Thursday	₹ ₹
Friday	₹ ₹ ₹ ₹
Saturday	₹ ₹ ₹ ₹ ₹ ₹ ₹
Sundday	₹ ₹
Each ₹ stands for ₹20.	

How much more money did Anuj spend on Friday than on Thursday?
(a) ₹ 30 (b) ₹ 70
(c) ₹ 20 (d) ₹ 90

29. How many lines and rays respectively are present in the given picture?

(a) 10, 19 (b) 1, 19
(c) 4, 19 (d) 1, 4

30. Which is the next figure in the given pattern?

(a)    (b) 

(c)    (d) 

31. The capacity of a small container is 400 mL and the capacity of a big container is 1500 mL. If Sumit uses 9 small containers and 2 big containers of water to fill up an empty tank, then what is the capacity of the tank?

(a) 5 L 200 mL (b) 6 L 600 mL
(c) 4 L 500 mL (d) 6 L 60 mL

32. In a game of 'spinning the wheel', it takes about 2 seconds for the pin in going from one month to the next month in anti-clockwise direction. If the wheel spins for about 30 seconds, then at which month the pin of the wheel stops?

(a) March (b) February
(c) November (d) January

33. If

Then, find the value of

(a) 58 (b) 42
(c) 35 (d) 43

34. State true or false and choose the correct option.

I. Area is expressed in unit length.
II. The measuring unit for area and perimeter is always same.
III. Triangle is a quadrilateral.
IV. If the side of a square park is 12 m, then its perimeter is 48 m.

	I	II	III	IV		I	II	III	IV
(a)	T	F	T	F	(b)	F	F	F	T
(c)	T	T	F	T	(d)	F	T	T	F

35. The circle chart shows the favourite hobbies of 120 girls of class 10.

$\frac{1}{3}$ of the girls like music and dance.

How many girls like dance, if 14 of them like music?

(a) 26 (b) 14
(c) 40 (d) 54

PRACTICE SET 02

1. The population of the city where Diana born is 145526. What is the population when rounded off to nearest thousand?

(a) 145000 (b) 145600
(c) 145500 (d) 146000

2. Look at the given numbers.

17, 18, 19, 16

Which two numbers should be selected from the above box, so that the following equation becomes true?

$\square \times \square = 342$

(a) 18, 16 (b) 17, 19
(c) 18, 19 (d) 17, 16

3. Tancy daily studies for few hours. She studied 6 hours on Monday as shown in the model.

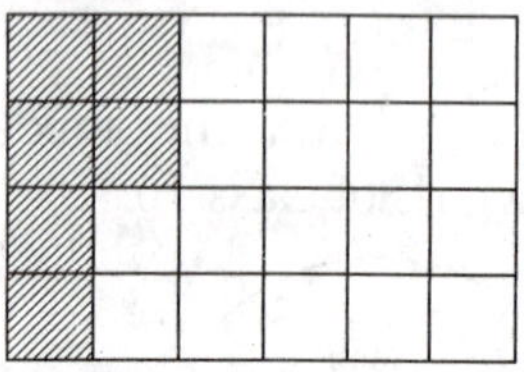

On Tuesday, she studied for more hours than on Monday. Which of the following fractions could represent the number of hours Tancy studied on Tuesday?

(a) $\frac{1}{6}$ (b) $\frac{1}{8}$
(c) $\frac{2}{4}$ (d) $\frac{1}{24}$

4. Which statement about $\frac{3}{4}$ and $\frac{9}{10}$ is true?

(a) $\frac{3}{4} = \frac{9}{10}$ because $4 - 3 = 1$ and $10 - 9 = 1$
(b) $\frac{3}{4} = \frac{9}{10}$ because $3 + 6 = 9$ and $4 + 6 = 10$
(c) $\frac{3}{4} < \frac{9}{10}$ because $3 < 9$ and $4 < 10$
(d) $\frac{3}{4} < \frac{9}{10}$ because $\frac{3}{4}$ is less than $\frac{4}{5}$ and $\frac{9}{10}$ is greater than $\frac{4}{5}$

5. Mia read 0.42 pages of a story book. How many pages Mia read, if the total number of pages is 100?

(a) 4.2 (b) 42
(c) 4 (d) 420

6. The total number of sugar packets of 300 g required to make 4.5 kg are

(a) 3 (b) 12 (c) 15 (d) 20

7. Which term means a figure that is formed by two rays or two line segments with a common end point?

(a) Vertex (b) Angle
(c) Edge (d) Intersecting lines

8. Gretta poured juice into a measuring container like the one shown. How much juice is in the container?

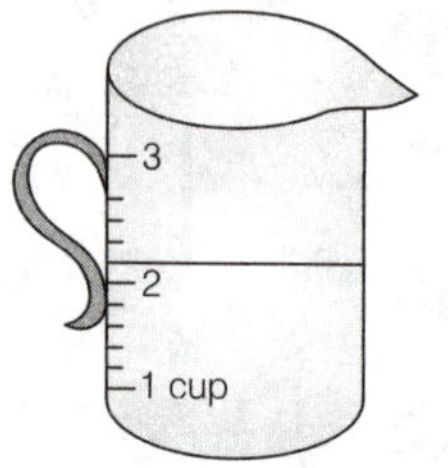

(a) $\frac{1}{2}$ cup (b) $2\frac{1}{5}$ cup
(c) $1\frac{1}{2}$ cup (d) $2\frac{1}{3}$ cup

9. A student is given the dimensions of rectangles *A*, *B* and *C*. Help him/her to find the rectangle(s) whose perimeter is greater than or equal to its area.

A : length = 8.5 cm, breadth = 2 cm

B : length = 5 cm, breadth = 4 cm

C : side = 4 cm

(a) *A* (b) *B*
(c) Both *A* and *C* (d) Both *B* and *C*

10. George bought 30 pencils and 20 pens for ₹ 5 and ₹ 10 each respectively. He wants to distribute it among the maximum number of children. What is the amount each child will pay to the Geroge?

(a) ₹ 50 (b) ₹ 15
(c) ₹ 35 (d) ₹ 40

11. How many letters in the English alphabet cannot be folded into halves?

(a) 10 (b) 11
(c) 12 (d) 13

12. Suman ordered some pizza for her friends. She surveyed toppings that they would like on their pizzas.

Toppings	Number of votes
Cheese	|||
Pepperoni	~~||||~~ |
Sausage	||||
Mushroom	–
Onion	||

What can Suman most likely conclude from her survey?

(a) Most of Suman's friend like cheese than pepperoni pizza
(b) Sausage is the group's second favourite type of pizza
(c) Suman needs to order only 1 onion pizza
(d) A pizza with both pepperoni and mushroom should be ordered

13. Austen has two piggy banks. In Ist bank, she collected coins and in 2nd bank, she collected notes.

The money in each piggy bank is shown below :

Piggy bank I

Piggy bank II

How much money Austen have in total when rounded off to nearest ten?

(a) ₹ 110 (b) ₹ 100
(c) ₹ 115 (d) ₹ 120

Directions (Q. Nos. 14 and 15) The following graph shows the number of spectators that were present at each event of olympic games. Use the graph to answer the questions.

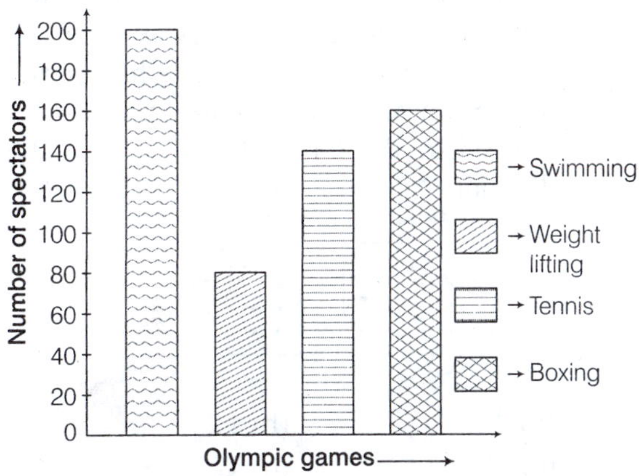

14. How many spectators were there at the boxing event?

(a) 140 (b) 130
(c) 160 (d) 180

15. The difference between the maximum and minimum number of spectators in these events is

(a) 100 (b) 80
(c) 60 (d) 120

16. Louisa has some candies in her bag. She can give an equal number of pieces of candy to 5, 3 or 2 people. Which number of pieces of candy could be in Louisa's bag?

(a) 12 (b) 20
(c) 30 (d) 45

17. Adira's birthday is coming. Her mom decided to throw a birthday party. There are 18 children who will come in her birthday party and each child will require 2 scoops of ice-creams. If Adira's mom can get 6 scoops of ice-creams out of every container, then how many containers will Adira's mom require?

(a) 3 (b) 4
(c) 6 (d) 9

18. Anouk is playing ludo with four of his friends. Each player throws two dice at a time, then add the numbers on dice and move the tokens forward. What is the maximum number of squares that can be jumped by the token throwing both the dice once?

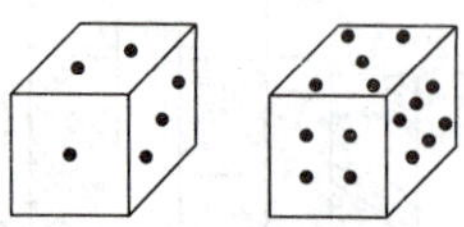

(a) 9 (b) 11
(c) 15 (d) 12

19. Here are some clues regarding a number.

I. It is an even number.
II. It is a multiple of 5 and factor of 10.
III. It is less than 27.

The number that fits in all the clues is

(a) 5 (b) 10
(c) 20 (d) 25

20. Which of the given figures has maximum number of obtuse angles?

(a) 
(b) 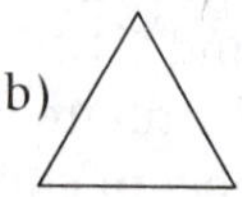
(c) 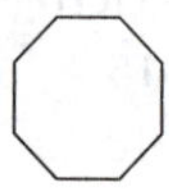
(d) 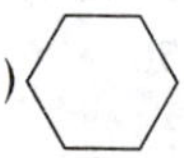

21. If the HCF of first two multiples of a number is one of numbers, then their LCM is

(a) same as HCF
(b) other number
(c) any one of the two numbers
(d) Cannot be determined

22. Daniel has a chart paper in which he puts his stamps. If the length and breadth of the chart paper is 13 cm and 8 cm respectively, then how many stamps could be placed inside the chart paper, if each stamp occupies an area of 2 cm^2?

(a) 50 (b) 52
(c) 48 (d) 54

23. Decode the word after arranging the decimal in decreasing order and choose the correct option.

1.25	3.98	4.84	6.53
+2.95	× 4	÷ 2	− 1.64
M	T	E	A

(a) MEAT (b) MATE
(c) TEAM (d) TAME

24. Joy wrote an expression below:

$$(8\times 2)\times 5$$

Which expression is equivalent to Joy's expression?

(a) $(8+2)\times 5$

(b) $(8\times 2)+5$

(c) $8\times(2\times 5)$

(d) $8\times(2\div 5)$

25. Allen is writing a poem. He writes 7 words on the first line, 12 words on the second line, 17 words on the third line. If the pattern continues in the same way, then how many words will Allen write on the eighth line?

(a) 42 (b) 37

(c) 47 (d) 34

26. Zandra joined the dance classes. Her teacher charges ₹ 150 for every class of one hour. If Zandra joined the classes on 15th April, 2015 and continued it till 19th June, then how much money does Zandra owe to her dance teacher, assuming that there are no extra classes and a holiday on Sunday?

April 2015

S	M	T	W	T	F	S
			1	2	3	4
5	6	7	8	9	10	11
12	13	14	15	16	17	18
19	20	21	22	23	24	25
26	27	28	29	30		

(a) ₹ 9900 (b) ₹ 9000

(c) ₹ 8550 (d) ₹ 11250

27. Which number replaces the question mark?

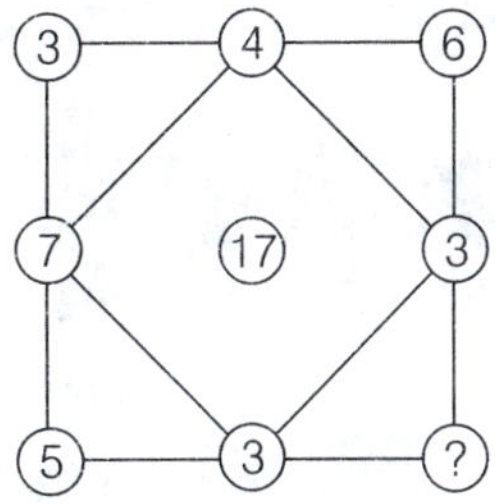

(a) 2 (b) 4

(c) 3 (d) 5

28. Eeva has climbed 15 stairs. She needs to climb a total of 25 stairs. The shaded region of which figure models the number of stairs Eeva has climbed out of the total number she needs to climb?

(a) 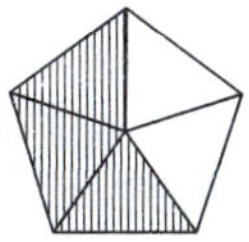

(b) 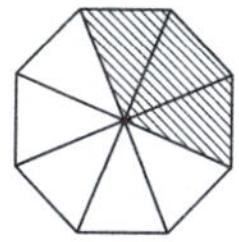

(c) 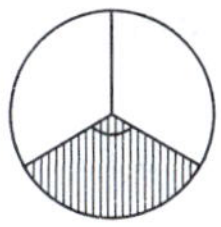

(d) 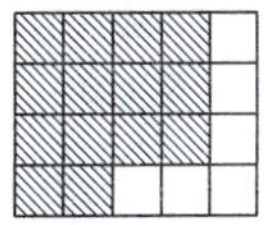

29. A farmer picked 795 tomatoes from his field and divided them equally into 35 bunches. How many tomatoes are in each bunch? Is there any tomatoes left out from packing?

(a) $Q=22, R=30$ (b) $Q=22, R=25$

(c) $Q=20, R=25$ (d) $Q=25, R=30$

30. Amit's weight is 64 kg and his brother is $1\frac{1}{4}$ times to his weight. What is the total weight of both of them?

(a) 144 kg (b) 100 kg

(c) 110 kg (d) 140 kg

31. Number of men and women in a city is given below

Man = 

Women = 

If  = 5 men and  = 7 women

How many women are more than men in the city?

(a) 5 (b) 1

(c) 6 (d) 3

32. The diagram below shows the travelling time of Michael from house to school and school to garden. If it is 6:20 am now, then at what time will he reach the garden, if he starts travelling from his home?

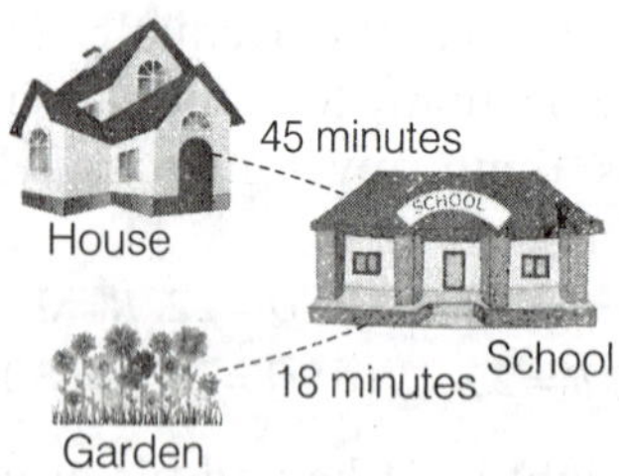

(a) 7 : 10 am (b) 6 : 55 am

(c) 7 : 15 am (d) 7 : 23 am

33. The diagram below has some numbers in the boxes. If the sum of numbers in each diagonal is equal, then find the value of *A*.

A		192
	248	
137		65

(a) 137 (b) 158

(c) 264 (d) 295

34. Robin folded a rectangular napkin along the dotted line as shown below. Find the difference between the perimeter of the napkin after folding and before folding.

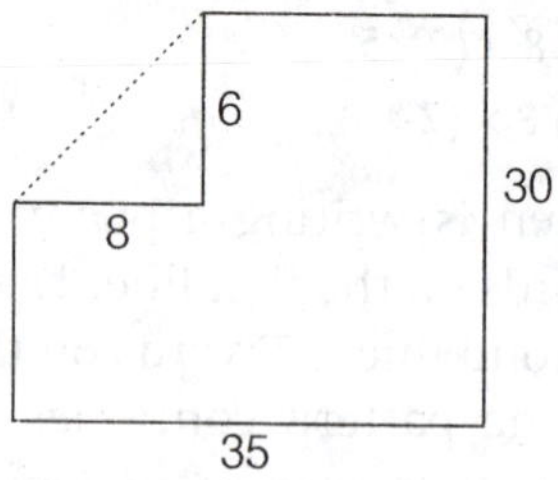

(a) 14 cm (b) 8 cm

(c) 2 cm (d) 0 cm

35. The given pictograph shows the record of the sale of oranges during a week by a fruit seller. Study the graph carefully and answer the following question.

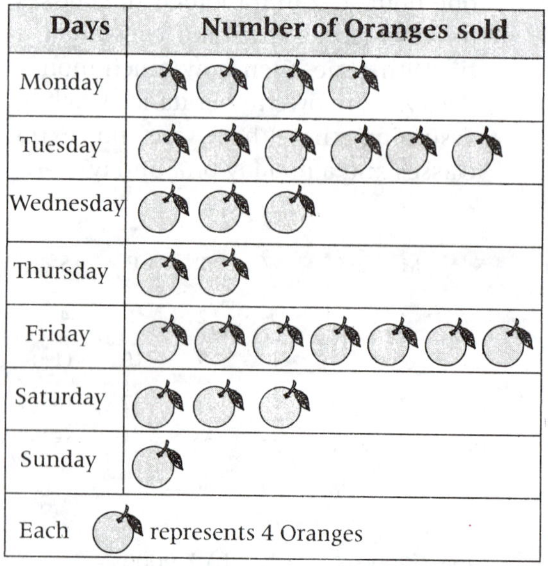

What fraction of the oranges were sold on Friday to the total number of oranges sold?

(a) $\frac{5}{26}$ (b) $\frac{7}{26}$

(c) $\frac{7}{54}$ (d) $\frac{3}{29}$

HINTS AND SOLUTIONS

1. Numbers

1. *(c)* Eighty six thousand four hundred can be written as 80000 + 6000 + 400 = 86400.

2. *(b)* 23456 = Twenty three thousand four hundred fifty six.

Hence, option (b) is correct.

3. *(c)* Successor of 67854398 = 67854399

Predecessor of 54677456 = 54677455

$\therefore$ Required difference

= 67854399 – 54677455 = 13176944

So, '2' does not appear in the required difference.

4. *(a)* V represents by the given figure.

So, V represents 5 in roman numeral.

5. *(c)* According to the question,

LIV	<	XCIX
(54)		(99)
XLIV	<	XLVI
(44)		(46)
CCV	>	XCV
(205)		(95)

Hence, option (c) is correct.

6. *(d)* Given,

Number of copies sold of All sports magazine

= MCCCLIII

= 1000+100+100+100+50+3 = 1353

Number of copies sold of Teenage magazine

= MCXXIII

= 1000+100+10+10+3 = 1123

Number of copies sold of Young people magazine = DXXIV = 500+10+10+4 = 524

Number of copies sold of Music time magazine

= DCCXLVIII

= 500+100+100+(50–10)+8 = 748

So, Music time magazine sold 748 copies which has 4 in tens place.

Hence, option (d) is correct.

7. *(a)* Face value of 9 in 26594325 = 9 and Place value of 9 in 26594325 = 90000

[$\because$ 9 is at ten thousand place]

$\therefore$ Required difference = 90000 – 9 = 89991

8. *(d)* In option (a), 100 ones $= 100 \times 1 = 100$

In option (b), 10 tens $= 10 \times 10 = 100$

In option (c), 1 hundred $= 1 \times 100 = 100$

In option (d), 100 tens $= 100 \times 10 = 1000$

So, option (d) is the odd one.

9. *(c)* Amount spent by three persons to buy household items = ₹ (1072 + 260 + 128)

= ₹ 1460

Now, $1460 = 1 \times 1000 + 4 \times 100 + 6 \times 10 + 0$

= 1 thousand + 4 hundred + 6 tens + 0 ones

Hence, there are 6 tens in the total amount spent by three persons.

10. *(a)* In option (a), 34 tens 47 ones

$= 34 \times 10 + 47 \times 1 = 340 + 47 = 387$

In option (b), 42 tens 7 ones $= 42 \times 10 + 7 \times 1$

$= 420 + 7 = 427$

In option (c), 41 tens 27 ones

$= 41 \times 10 + 27 \times 1 = 410 + 27 = 437$

In option (d), 82 tens 22 ones

$= 82 \times 10 + 22 \times 1 = 820 + 22 = 842$

So, option (a) does not have digit 4 in it.

11. *(c)* According to the question,

(i) 5 tens $= 5 \times 10 = 50$

(ii) 8 thousand $= 8 \times 1000 = 8000$

(iii) 2 ones

(iv) 6 ten thousand $= 6 \times 10000 = 60000$

(v) 0 ones $= 0 \times 1 = 0$

So, mystery number

= 60000 + 8000 + 50 + 2 = 68052

12. *(b)* $9243 = 9 \times 1000 + 2 \times 100 + 4 \times 10 + 3 \times 1$

= 9000 + 200 + 40 + 3

= 9 thousand + 2 hundred + 4 tens + 3 ones

So this is shown by abacus in option (b).

Hence, option (b) is correct.

13. (*b*) The sum of the given amount

$= 435900 + 455500 = ₹\ 891400$

Here, '4' is at hundred place, so its place value in ₹ 891400 is 400.

14. (*a*) Now, considering option (a),

In 80658, first and last digits are same. 5 at tens place and 6 at hundreds place and sum of all digits equal to 27.

So, 80658, satisfy the all given conditions.

Hence, option (a) is correct.

15. (*a*) $596280 = 500000 + \boxed{90000} + \boxed{6000} + \boxed{200} + 80$

So, 90000, 6000 and 200 are the three numbers which fill the boxes correctly.

Hence, option (a) is correct.

16. (*b*) The number should be greater than 1898 but less than 2098.

$1836 < 1898$

$1899 > 1898$ and $1899 < 2098$

$1888 < 1898$

$1829 < 1898$

So, option (b) satisfies the given condition.

Hence, option (b) is correct.

17. (*c*) Considering option (c),

$57324 > 57234 > 43275 > 34275$

So, this is correct descending order.

Hence option (c) is correct.

18. (*c*) Since, the ascending order of given number is $6876 < 6887 < 6909 < 6916$

So, 6876 is the least number of pages in the given table.

Hence, Sonia read the least number of pages in the month of March.

19. (*c*) Among the given options, only 453364 when rounded off to nearest 100 gives 453400, since $64 > 50$.

So, actual population of Bolivia is 453364.

20. (*d*) **Statement 1** : Rounded off digit = 6

Digit right to 6 is $6 > 5$.

∴ 5466 when rounded off to nearest tens gives 5470.

So, statements 1 is false.

Statement 2 : Rounded off digit = 4

Digit right to 4 is $6 > 5$.

∴ 41464 when rounded off to nearest hundreds gives 41500.

So, statements 2 is false.

Hence, both statements 1 and 2 are false.

21. (*b*) Here, the required number has 5 digits.

i.e., it will be of the form

Ten th	Th	Hundred	Tens	Ones
I	II	III	IV	V

To make the smallest number using the given digits. The smallest digits will be put at the highest place and so on.

'0' cannot be used on the ten thousand place.

Now, among 2, 3, 6, 7 we have 2 as the smallest digit. So, 2 will take the ten thousand place.

$\underset{\text{I}}{\underline{2}}\ \underset{\text{II}}{\underline{\ \ }}\ \underset{\text{III}}{\underline{\ \ }}\ \underset{\text{IV}}{\underline{\ \ }}\ \underset{\text{V}}{\underline{\ \ }}$

Now, IInd place will have smallest digit among 3, 0, 6, 7. So, '0' will come at IInd place.

Similarly, IIIrd digit = 3,

IVth digit = 6

and Vth digit = 7

∴ The number formed = 20367, which is an odd number.

22. (*a*) The smallest 5-digits number by the given digits = 20456

And the greatest 5-digits number by the given digits = 65420

So, required difference

$= 65420 - 20456 - = 44964$

23. (*a*) 926543 —Successor of 926542

10000 — Smallest 5-digit number

962540 — Place value of 2 is 2000

100000 — 100039 when rounded off to nearest 100

So, A→ (iv); B→(i); C→(ii); D→(iii)

Hence, option (a) is correct.

24. (*b*)

I. One crore is an 8-digit number, since 1 crore = 10000000

II. Successor of largest 4-digit number (9999) $= 9999 + 1 = 10000$ = Smallest 5-digit number.
III. 0 number has no roman numeral.
IV. Difference between successor and predecessor of a number is always 2.

So, I→(i); II.→(v); III.→(iv); IV→(vi)

Hence, option (b) is correct

25. *(c)*
(i) **True,** since in 380, we have $80 > 50$, so it will be rounded off to next nearest hundred.
(ii) **False,** CCXLV $= (100 + 100) + (50 - 10) + 5$
$= 200 + 40 + 5 = 245$
(iii) **False,** smallest 4-digit number that can be formed by using the digits 3, 5, 8, 0 is 3058.
(iv) **True,** largest 4-digit number = 9999
Smallest 4-digit number = 1000
∴ Required sum $= 9999 + 1000 = 10999$
Hence, option (c) is correct

2. Addition and Subtraction

1. *(a)* The sum of numbers.
$= 35469 + 23400 + 10101 = 68970$

2. *(d)* In option (a), XIV + V $= 14 + 5 = 19 \neq 20$
In option (b), X + XI $= 10 + 11 = 21 \neq 19$
In option (c), XI + XI $= 11 + 11 = 22 \neq 21$
In option (d), XI + XII $= 11 + 12 = 23$
Hence, option (d) is correctly matched.

3. *(b)* The given pattern is as follows
$P = 315 + 622 = 937$
[A number is distribute in two numbers]
$Q = P + 949 = 937 + 949 = 1886$
Hence, option (b) is correct.

4. *(c)* The total amount that Ria spent
= ₹1457 + ₹ 643 = ₹ 2100

5. *(b)* Total marks obtained in all the five subjects
$= 48 + 36 + 47 + 22 + 37$
$= 190$
So, 190 is closest to 200.

6. *(c)* Given,
Value of old fridge = ₹ 3250
and money paid by Tanvi = ₹ 6329
∴ Cost of TV that Tanvi bought
= ₹ 6329 + ₹ 3250 = ₹ 9579

7. *(b)* Given, number of pennies in bag 1 = 621
Number of pennies in bag 2 = 273
Number of pennies in bag 3 = 442
Number of pennies in bag 4 = 385
∴Total number of pennies John had
$= 621 + 273 + 442 + 385 = 1721$
Rounded off to nearest hundred, we get
Total $= 1700$ $(21 < 50)$
So, 1721 will be rounded off to 1700.

8. *(c)* Total distance covered by Sonia
= 46 km + 46 km + 84 km + 84 km
= 260 km
Hence, option (c) is correct.

9. *(d)* $? - 5 = 95$
∴ Minuend $= 95 + 5 = 100$
Hence, option (d) is correct.

10. *(d)* According to the question,
$3075 - 100 = 2975$
Hence, option (d) is correct.

11. *(b)* D − XXX − LX $= 500 - 30 - 60$
$= 500 - 90 = 410$

12. *(d)* According to the question,

$$\begin{array}{r} \boxed{5}\ 8\ 6\ 3\ \boxed{3} \\ -\ 3\ \boxed{2}\ 2\ \boxed{1}\ 2 \\ \hline 2\ 6\ \boxed{4}\ 2\ 1 \end{array}$$

∴ $P = 5$, $Q = 4$, $R = 1$, $S = 2$ and $T = 3$
So, $(P + T + Q) - (R + S)$
$= (5 + 3 + 4) - (1 + 2)$
$= 12 - 3 = 9$

13. *(b)*The following pattern is as follows :
$A = 700 - 25 = 675$
$B = 600 - 25 = 575$
$C = 500 - 25 = 475$
$D = 200 - 25 = 175$

14. (a) Given,

$$\begin{array}{r} 42859 \\ -14X26 \\ \hline 27933 \\ \hline \end{array}$$

$\Rightarrow$ $42859 - 27933 = 14X\,26$

$\Rightarrow$ $14926 = 14X\,26$

On comparing both sides, we get X = 9

15. (c) Given,

$$\begin{array}{r} 27933 \\ -11Y9 \\ \hline 26774 \end{array}$$

$\Rightarrow$ $27933 - 26774 = 11Y9$

$\Rightarrow$ $1159 = 11Y9$

On comparing both sides, we get

Y = 5

16. (b) The following pattern is as follows :

$A = 10 - 5 = 5$

$B = 1100 - 75 = 1025$

$C = 75 - 15 = 60$

$D = 15 - A = 15 - 5 = 10$

Hence, option (b) is correct.

17. (b) Sum of 1264 and 427 = 1691

Sum of 542 and 178 = 720

$\therefore$ Required difference = 1691 − 720

= 971

So, sum of 1264 and 427 is 971 more than the sum of 542 and 178.

18. (b) Given, Sum of two numbers = 17643

One number = 6689

$\therefore$ Other number = 17643 − 6689 = 10954

19. (b) Plants planted in Delhi = 6598

Plants planted in Uttar Pradesh = 2593

$\therefore$ Required difference = (6598 − 2593) = 4005

Hence, 4005 more plants are planted in Delhi.

20. (a) Cost price of a mobile phone = ₹ 3021

Cost price of another mobile phone = ₹ 2136

$\therefore$ Required difference = ₹ 3021 − ₹ 2136

= ₹ 885

21. (c) Account opened with an amount = ₹ 4000

Amount deposit after one month = ₹ 5276

and amount deposit next month = ₹ 3274

Total amount in his account

₹ 4000 + ₹ 5276 + ₹ 3274 = ₹ 12550

Amount withdraw from account by him

= ₹ 5000

$\therefore$ Remaining amount

= Total money − Withdrawl money

= ₹ 12550 − ₹ 5000

= ₹ 7550

22. (b) Total passengers in the train

= 482 − 76 + 46 = 452

23. (a) Required dozens of apples

= 400 − 67 − 23 = 310

24. (a) Given,

Cost of 2 doremon = ₹ 684

$\Rightarrow$ Cost of 1 doremon = ₹ 684 ÷ 2 = ₹ 342

Cost of 2 scooters and 1 doremon = ₹ 1986

$\Rightarrow$ Cost of 2 scooters

= ₹ 1986 − Cost of 1 doremon

= ₹ 1986 − ₹ 342

= ₹ 1644

$\therefore$ Cost of 1 scooter = ₹ 1644 ÷ 2 = ₹ 822

Cost of 1 car and 1 scooter = ₹ 2385

$\Rightarrow$ Cost of 1 car = ₹ 2385 − Cost of 1 scooter

= ₹ 2385 − ₹ 822 = ₹ 1563

$\therefore$ Cost of 3 scooters + Cost of 3 doremon + Cost of 2 cars

= 3 × ₹ 822 + 3 × ₹ 342 + 2 × ₹ 1563

= ₹ 2466 + ₹ 1026 + ₹ 3126

= ₹ 6618

25. (a) False, 97 + 87 + 77 = 261

False, we use subtraction when we find how many things are left.

True, 43496 − 27999 = 15497

False, Addition is used to find out the total amount.

3. Multiplication and Division

1. *(d)* 3×4 means, the figure having 3 rows and 4 columns.

Hence, option (d) figure is the correct answer.

2. *(a)* Given,

number of pearls in each Jewellery box = 5

Also, the number of jewellery box = 8

$\therefore$ According to the question, $5 \times 8 = 40$

$\therefore$ Hence, option (a) is correct.

3. *(c)* After observing the pattern, we can see

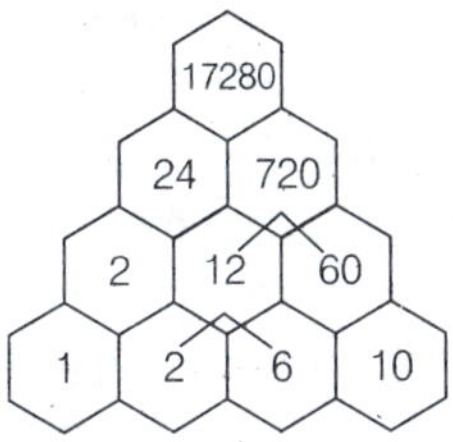

$1 \times 2 = 2$

$2 \times 6 = \boxed{12}$

$6 \times 10 = 60$

$2 \times 12 = 24$

$12 \times 60 = \boxed{720}$

$24 \times 720 = 17280$

Hence, option (c) is correct.

4. *(b)* After observing the pattern, we can see

$9 \times 8 = 72$

$9 \times 3 = 27$

$3 \times 4 = 12$

Similarly, $8 \times 4 = \boxed{32}$

So, the missing number is 32.

5. *(d)* Numbers on a telephone keypad are 1, 2, 3, 4, 5, 6, 7, 8, 9, 0.

We know that, any number multiplied by 0 is 0 itself.

$\therefore$ Product of all the numbers on a telephone keypad

$= 1 \times 2 \times 3 \times 4 \times 5 \times 6 \times 7 \times 8 \times 9 \times 0 = 0$

6. *(a)* Option (a), $23 \times 18 = 414$

Option (b), $52 \times 22 = 1144$

Option (c), $44 \times 26 = 1144$

Option (d), $104 \times 11 = 1144$

Except option (a) all other options have product equal to 1144.

7. *(b)* Number of tickets Aryan has = 132

Number of people that can use 1 ticket = 6

$\therefore$ Total number of people that can use 132 tickets $= 132 \times 6 = 792$

8. *(d)* The court has 72 rows and 50 seats in each row.

$\therefore$ Total number of seats in the court $= 72 \times 50$

$= 3600$

9. *(d)* According to the question there are four people, Sahil, Johny, Devansh and Sonal.

Each of them have 120 play cards.

So, total number of cards $= 120 \times 4 = 480$

10. *(c)* Number of goats in grazing field = 60

Total number of legs of goats $= 60 \times 4 = 240$

[$\because$ Each goat has 4 legs]

Number of deers in grazing field = 30

Total number of legs of deers $= 30 \times 4 = 120$

[$\because$ Each deer has 4 legs]

Number of children in grazing field = 10

Total number of legs of children $= 10 \times 2 = 20$

[$\because$ Each child has 2 legs]

$\therefore$ Total number of legs $= 240 + 120 + 20 = 380$

11. *(d)* If Cody throws, all the dart on circle with score 5, then score of Cody $= 5 \times 3 = 15$

If Cody throws all the dart on circle with score 6, then score of Cody $= 6 \times 3 = 18$

If Cody throws all the dart on circle with score 7, then score of Cody $= 7 \times 3 = 21$

So, 23 cannot be the score of Cody.

12. *(b)* Louisa has 30 stickers, first we will find the stickers for each day.

Days	Martin	Louisa
1	4	6
2	$4 \times 2 = 8$	$6 \times 2 = 12$
3	$4 \times 3 = 12$	$6 \times 3 = 18$
4	$4 \times 4 = 16$	$6 \times 4 = 24$
5	$4 \times 5 = 20$	$6 \times 5 = 30$

From the given table, it is clear that Martin had 20 stickers when Louisa had 30 stickers.

13. *(a)* According to the question,

there are 5 rows in which these are 4 triangles in each row.

So, there are $5 \times 4 = 20$ triangles.

$\therefore$ It can be written as either $20 \div 4 = 5$

or, $20 \div 5 = 4$

Hence, option (a) is correct.

14. *(a)* According to the pattern,

$\boxed{26000} \div 13000 = 2$

$26000 \div 1300 = \boxed{20}$

$\boxed{26000} \div 130 = 200$

$26000 \div 13 = 2000$

Hence, option (a) is correct.

15. *(b)* Given,

12) 9 3 7 9 5 (7 [8] 1 [6]
−84
[9]7
−96
1 9
− 1 2
[7]5
− 7 2
3

Here, $L = 8$, $M = 9$, $N = 7$, $P = 6$

$\therefore (L + M + N) \div P = (8 + 9 + 7) \div 6 = 24 \div 6 = 4$

$\therefore$ Hence, option, (b) is correct.

16. *(a)* Given,

$$72 \div h = 6 \quad \Rightarrow \quad \frac{72}{h} = 6$$

$$\Rightarrow \quad h = \frac{72}{6} \quad \Rightarrow \quad h = 72 \div 6 = 12$$

So, Arnab has 12 horses.

17. *(a)* Total number of burgers = 534

Burger in each packet = 6

$\therefore$ Total number of packets required

$= 534 \div 6 = 89$

18. *(a)* Number of mangoes that each friend get

$= 13 \div 5$

5) 13 (2
−10
3

$\therefore$ Quotient = 2, Remainder = 3

Each friend get 2 mangoes and 3 mangoes are left over.

19. *(d)* For verification, we have the rule

Dividend = Divisor × Quotient + Remainder

Here, Dividend = 188, Divisor = 7,

Quotient = 26 and Remainder = 6

In option (a), $(6 \times 26) + 7 = 163$

In option (b), $(26 \times 7) + 7 = 189$

In option (c), $(7 + 26) \times 6 = 198$

In option (d), $(7 \times 26) + 6 = 188$

So, option (d) is the correct answer.

20. *(b)* According to the question,

Total number of bicycles = 27

Number of persons who want to sell bicycles = 2

Number of bicycles per person = $27 \div 2$

2) 27 (13
−2↓
7
− 6
1

$\therefore$ Equal number of bicycles that each person has = 13

So, 1 bicycle will be left over.

21. *(b)* A.

12) 281 (23
−24↓
4 1
− 3 6
5

$\therefore$ Quotient = 23

Remainder = 5

B.

```
7 ) 8357 (1193
   -7
    13
    -7
     65
    -63
      27
     -21
      ×6
```

∴Quotient = 1193

Remainder = 6

C.

```
7 ) 8357 (1193
   -7↓
    13
    -7↓
     65
    -63↓
      27
     -21
      ×6
```

∴Quotient = 1493

Remainder = 3

D.

```
9 ) 1726 (191
   -9↓
    82
   -81↓
     16
     -9
      7
```

∴Quotient = 191

Remainder = 7

So, A→ (ii); B→ (i); C→ (iv); D→ (iii)

22. (*a*)

(i) False, $720 \div 720 = 1$

(ii) True, when 0 is divided by any number the result will e 0.

(iii) True, $8000 \div 2 = 4000$

23. (*c*)

I. $94 \times 6 = 564$ and $6 \times 94 = 564$

$\therefore \quad 94 \times 6 = 6 \times 94$

II. $13 \times 9 + 6 = 123$

and $6 \times 9 + 13 = 67 \Rightarrow 123 > 67$

$\therefore \quad 13 \times 9 + 6 > 6 \times 9 + 13$

III. $0 \div 83 = 0$ and $83 \div 1 = 83 \quad \Rightarrow \quad 0 < 83$

$\therefore \quad 0 \div 83 < 83 \div 1$

Hence, option (c) is correct.

4. Multiples and Factors

1. (*a*) 1 is the factor of every number.

2. (*d*) Factors of 72 are 1, 2, 3, 4, 6, 8, 9, 12, 18, 24, 36, 72.

So, number of factors of 72 = 12.

3. (*b*) Multiples of 20 (between 10 and 190) are 20, 40, 60, 80, 100, 120, 140, 160, 180

So, total number of multiples = 9

4. (*d*) To find the multiples of 9, first we recall the table of 9.

$9 \times 1 = 9$ $9 \times 2 = 18$

$9 \times 3 = 27$ $9 \times 4 = 36$

$9 \times 5 = 45$ $9 \times 6 = 54$

$9 \times 7 = 63$ $9 \times 8 = 72$

$9 \times 9 = 81$

So, it is clear that the numbers shown in option (d), i.e., 9, 18 and 45 are the multiples of 9.

5. (*c*) Given activity is helpful to understand concept of multiples and factors.

6. (*a*) $\because \; 56 = 7 \times 8$ and $8 = 4 \times 2$

$\therefore \qquad x = 8$

7. (*b*) According to the question, $45 = 5 \times 9$

and $54 = 6 \times 9$

So, 9 is a single digit odd number.

8. (*a*)

I. 3 is the smallest odd prime number.

II. A number having more than 2 factors is called a composite number.

III. 1 is neither a prime number nor a composite number.

IV. The numbers having factors 2 and 3 also have factor 6.

Hence, option (a) is correct.

9. (*a*) We have, factors of 10 are 1, 2, 5 and 10.

Factors of 12 are 1, 2, 3, 4, 6 and 12.

Factors of 6 = 1, 2, 3, 6

Factors of 8 = 1, 2, 4, 8

Factors of 15 = 1, 3, 5, 15

From above factors, it is clear that 12 has 2 more factors than 10.

12 and 10 have 2 common factors, i.e., 1 and 2. The smallest possible value of X is 12.

10. *(b)* Number of water bottles collected by Anna $= 8$

Number of water bottles Raj collected

$= \text{Twice as collected by Anna} = 2 \times 8 = 16$

So, Raj had collected total 16 bottles.

11. *(d)* From the given expression, it is clear that 42 is 3 times as many as 14.

12. *(b)* The year which is divisible by 2 and 5 and also closest to the 21st century.

1999 is not divisible by 2 and 5. 1990 is divisible by 2 and 5 both and also closest to the 21st century.

1995 is not divisible by 2 and 1998 is not divisible by 5.

Hence, option (b) is correct.

13. *(d)* Every number is a factor and multiple of itself.

14. *(b)* Numbers between 20 and 30 are 21, 22, 23, 24, 25, 26, 27, 28, 29 and multiple of 4 are 24 and 28. When 24 is divided by 8, it leaves no remainder.

Hence, the required number is 24.

15. *(c)* According to the question,

6th multiple of $7 = 6 \times 7 = 42$

3rd multiple of $9 = 3 \times 9 = 27$

11th multiple of $12 = 11 \times 12 = 132$

$\therefore$ Required result $= 132 - (42 + 27)$

$= 132 - 69 = 63$

16. *(c)* The smallest number which is a common multiple of 6 and 8 but not of 9 is 24.

$\therefore$ Required result $= 7 \times 5 + 24 = 35 + 24 = 59$

17. *(c)* Only ₹ 432, i.e., the price of Computer Olympiad book is a multiple of 3 among all the four prices of books, since $432 = 3 \times 144$

18. *(b)*

(a) Max is correct, as there are only 4 multiples of 8, i.e., 80, 40, 48, 24.

$\because$ $80 = 8 \times 10$, $40 = 8 \times 5$; $48 = 8 \times 6$, $24 = 8 \times 3$

(b) Jeniffer is not correct, since 17, 11 and 2 are prime numbers.

(c) Rocky is correct, since (40, 11) are coprime numbers.

(d) Anjie is correct, since 11 is not an even number.

19. *(c)* From Statement I, among the given options (a) and (b) are not even numbers.

From Statement II, options (c) and (d) both are multiples of 6 and 7.

From Statement III, only 42 has total of 8 factors, i.e., 1, 2, 3, 6, 7, 14, 21, 42.

Hence, option (c) is correct.

20. *(c)* According to the question,

3rd multiple of $11 = 11 \times 3 = 33$

Factors of 8 are 1, 2, 4 and 8.

Factors of 10 are 1, 2, 5 and 10.

Common factors of 8 and 10 are 1 and 2.

Their difference $= 2 - 1 = 1$

So, required sum $= 33 + 1 = 34$

21. (b) Multiples of 7 are 7, 14, 21 and 28.

$7 = 1 \times 7;$

$24 = 2 \times 2 \times 2 \times 3$

$\therefore$ HCF (7, 24) $= 1$

$14 = 2 \times 7$; $24 = 2 \times 2 \times 2 \times 3$

$\therefore$ HCF (14, 24) $= 2$

$21 = 3 \times 7;$

$24 = 2 \times 2 \times 2 \times 3$

$\therefore$ HCF (21, 24) $= 3$

and $28 = 2 \times 2 \times 7$

$24 = 2 \times 2 \times 2 \times 3$

$\therefore$ HCF (28, 24) $= 4$

So, date chosen by Raghav $= 14$

[$\because$ 14 is multiples of 7 and the HCF of (14, 24) $= 2$]

22. *(a)* Since, the day after which both the trucks will visit together $=$ LCM (4, 5)

$= 4 \times 5 = 20.$

So, both the trucks will visit after 20 days.

23. *(b)* Steps are as follow:

II. Greatest 4-digit number is 9999.

III. LCM of 15, 25, 40 and 75 is 600.

I. On dividing 9999 by 600, the remainder is 399.

IV. Number is (9999 – 399) = 9600.

So, the correct order is II, III, I, IV.

Hence, option (b) is correct

24. *(d)*

I. True, coprimes numbers have only one common factor, i.e., 1.

II. False, least prime number is 2.

III. True.

IV. True.

Hence, option (d) is correct

25. *(b)*

I. LCM (15, 30)

$15 = 3 \times 5$ and $30 = 2 \times 3 \times 5$

So, LCM (15, 30) $= 2 \times 3 \times 5 = 30$

II. LCM (8, 16)

$8 = 2 \times 2 \times 2$ and $16 = 2 \times 2 \times 2 \times 2$

So, LCM (8,16) $= 2 \times 2 \times 2 \times 2 = 16$, which is a factor of 64.

III. Factors of 2 = 1, 2

Factors of 15 = 1, 3, 5, 15

$\therefore$ Required sum = 27

IV. HCF (24, 6)

$24 = 2 \times 2 \times 2 \times 3$ and $6 = 2 \times 3$

So, HCF (24, 6) $= 2 \times 3 = 6$

$\therefore$ I $\rightarrow$ (iv); II. $\rightarrow$ (iii); IV. $\rightarrow$ (ii); IV. $\rightarrow$ (i)

5. Fractions

1. *(d)* In option (a), one-quarter $= \frac{1}{4}$ part is shaded.

In option (b), $2/8 = \frac{1}{4}$ part is shaded.

In option (c), $2/8 = \frac{1}{4}$ part is shaded.

In option (d), $\frac{4}{12} = \frac{1}{3}$ part is shaded.

So, option (d) figure does not show one-quarter shaded.

2. *(a)* Fraction of the shaded portion of given image $= \frac{5}{8}$

Fraction of unshaded portion in option (a), $= \frac{5}{8}$

Hence, option (a) is correct.

3. *(d)* Total number of triangles = 16

Given shaded fraction $= \frac{2}{4}$

So, the number of triangles shaded to get $\frac{2}{4}$

shaded fraction $= \frac{2}{4} \times 16 = 8$

$\therefore$ Number of triangle already shades = 10

Hence, number of triangle must be unshaded

$= 10 - 8 = 2$

4. *(c)* First see the word 'EDUCATION' select the alphabet having curved lines

i.e. D, U, C, O = 4

Total Alphabet = 9

Required fraction $= \frac{4}{9}$

5. *(c)* If we divide numerator and denominator both by 13, then $\frac{26 \div 13}{65 \div 13} = \frac{2}{5}$.

If we divide both $\frac{104}{117}$ by 13, then it will become $\frac{8}{9}$.

Similarly, if we divide $\frac{91 \div 13}{143 \div 13} = \frac{7}{11}$

6. *(b)* We have,

I. $\frac{56}{9} = 6\frac{2}{9}$ II. $\frac{37}{9} = 4\frac{1}{9}$

III. $\frac{23}{9} = 2\frac{5}{9}$ IV. $\frac{43}{9} = 4\frac{7}{9}$

So, I $\rightarrow$ (iv); II. $\rightarrow$ (i); III. $\rightarrow$ (ii); (iv) $\rightarrow$ (iii)

7. *(c)* Given that sum of diagonals are equal.

Thus, $\frac{2}{19} + \frac{3}{19} + \frac{6}{19} = \frac{4}{19} + \frac{3}{19} + x$

$\Rightarrow \frac{11}{19} = \frac{7}{19} + x$

$\therefore x = \frac{11}{19} - \frac{7}{19} = \frac{4}{19}$

8. (*b*) P represents $= 2\frac{6}{10} = \frac{26}{10}$

Q represents $= 4\frac{3}{10} = \frac{43}{10}$

$\therefore \quad Q - P = \frac{43}{10} - \frac{26}{10} = \frac{17}{10}$

9. (*d*) Given, $\frac{7}{X} - 1\frac{3}{10} = \frac{1}{10}$

$\Rightarrow \quad \frac{7}{X} - \frac{13}{10} = \frac{1}{10} \Rightarrow \frac{7}{X} = \frac{1}{10} + \frac{13}{10}$

$\Rightarrow \quad \frac{7}{X} = \frac{14}{10} \Rightarrow \frac{7}{X} = \frac{7}{5}$

$\therefore X = 5$

10. (*c*) Given, $3\frac{3}{4} + 2\frac{5}{6} = x\frac{y}{z}$

$\Rightarrow \frac{15}{4} + \frac{17}{6} = x\frac{y}{z}$

$\Rightarrow x\frac{y}{z} = \frac{45+34}{12} = \frac{79}{12}$

$\Rightarrow x\frac{y}{z} = 6\frac{7}{12}$

On comparing, $x = 6, y = 7, z = 12$

Hence, option (c) is correct.

11. (*c*) Total number of frogs $= 15$

Number of frogs hopped away $= 11$

Number of frogs left behind $= 15 - 11 = 4$

$\therefore$ Required fraction $= \frac{4}{15}$

12. (*a*) Alphabets made up of straight lines $= 15$ [first write all the alphabets on rough paper, then select the alphabets having only straight lines]

A, E, F, H, I, K, L, M, N, T, V, W, X, Y, Z.

Total number of alphabets = 26

$\therefore \quad$ Required fraction $= \frac{15}{26}$

13. (*b*) Let total capacity of jar be 1.

Then, fraction of jar filled with milk $= \frac{1}{5}$

Fraction of jar filled with water $= \frac{2}{5}$

So, fraction of jar remains empty

$= 1 - \left(\frac{1}{5} + \frac{2}{5}\right) = 1 - \frac{3}{5} = \frac{2}{5}$

14. (*b*) Considering option (b),

Number of matches played by $B = 6$

Number of matches won by $B = 3$

So, it is clear that number of matches won by B are exactly half the matches he played.

Hence, option (b) is correct.

15. (*b*)Given, $A + B = \frac{1}{3}$

and $A + B + C = \frac{3}{4} \Rightarrow \frac{1}{3} + C = \frac{3}{4}$

$\Rightarrow C = \frac{3}{4} - \frac{1}{3} = \frac{3\times3}{4\times3} - \frac{1\times4}{3\times4} = \frac{9}{12} - \frac{4}{12} = \frac{5}{12}$

16. (*a*) Apples eaten by Shalini on Tuesday $= \frac{1}{9}$

Apples eaten by Shalini on Wednesday $= \frac{2}{9}$

Apples eaten by Shalini on Thursday $= \frac{2}{9}$

Remaining fraction of apples $= 1 - \left(\frac{1}{9} + \frac{2}{9} + \frac{2}{9}\right)$

$= 1 - \frac{5}{9} = \frac{9-5}{9} = \frac{4}{9}$

17. (*a*) Given price of meal = ₹ 84

Discount coupon $= \frac{3}{4}$

Discount available $= \frac{3}{4}$ of $84 = \frac{3}{4} \times 84 =$ ₹ 63

$\therefore$ Price of meal = 84 − 63 = ₹ 21

18. (*b*) Sum of unshaded fractions

$= \frac{3}{4} + \frac{3}{4} = \frac{6}{4} = \frac{3}{2} = 1\frac{1}{2}$

19. (*a*) Quantity of sugar Nishant bought $= 3\frac{6}{12}$ kg

$= \frac{42}{12}$ kg $= \frac{7}{2}$ kg

Quantity of Sugar Aman bought

$= \left(\frac{7}{2} - \frac{1}{2}\right)$ kg $= \frac{7-1}{2}$ kg $= \frac{6}{2}$ kg $= 3$ kg

20. (*b*) Given,

 +  +  $= \frac{17}{12}$ ... (i)

Also,  +  $= \frac{7}{6}$ ... (ii)

From (i) and (ii), we have

$\frac{7}{6} +$  $= \frac{17}{12}$

$\Rightarrow$  $= \frac{17}{12} - \frac{7}{6} = \frac{17}{12} - \frac{7\times 2}{6\times 2} = \frac{17}{12} - \frac{14}{12} = \frac{3}{12}$

Also,  −  $= \frac{5}{12} \Rightarrow$  $- \frac{3}{12} = \frac{5}{12}$

$\therefore$  $= \frac{5}{12} + \frac{3}{12} = \frac{8}{12} = \frac{2}{3}$

21. (*c*) Number of males left the stadium

$= \frac{2}{5} \times 2000 = 800$

Remaining males in the stadium

$= 2000 - 800 = 1200$

Number of female left the stadium

$= \frac{2}{10} \times 2500 = 500$

Remaining females in the stadium

$= 2500 - 500 = 2000$

Total persons left in stadium after 2 h
= Remaining males + Remaining female
$= 1200 + 2000 = 3200$

6. Measurements

1. (*c*) The length of the given object is 3 cm and 3 mm which is equal to 3.3 cm or 3 cm 3 mm.

2. (*b*) Here, AD = 3 cm, EF = 1 cm, HJ = 2 cm

$\therefore$ AD + EF + HJ = 3 cm + 1 cm + 2 cm = 6 cm
and AF = 5 cm, DJ = 6 cm, *CG* = 4 cm,
EJ = 5 cm

Hence, AD + EF + HJ = DJ

3. (*c*) Measure of 1 hand = 4 inch

Height of horse = 14 hands

Measure of 14 hands = 14 × 4 inch = 56 inch

$\therefore$ Height of a horse = 56 inch

4. (*b*) The given distance between Aaron and his grandma's house = 5300 m

Length of long route = 9.2 km

[$\because$ 1 km = 1000 m]

= 9.2 × 1000 m = 9200 m

$\therefore$ Required difference = 9200 m − 5300 m

= 3900 m = (3900 ÷ 1000) km = 3.9 km

5. (*c*) Since, in border *X*, 16 small rope piece of 1 cm needed to make the border. In the same way, 10 small rope piece of 1 cm needed to make the border *Y*. Hence, length of the border *Y* = 10 × 1 cm = 10 cm

6. (*b*) Length of Kelsey's pencil box = 16 cm

According to the question,

Length of Hanna's pencil box

= Length of Kelsey's pencil box − 4 cm

= 16 cm − 4 cm = 12 cm

and length of Mark's pencil box

= Length of Hanna's pencil box + 2 cm

= 12 cm + 2 cm = 14 cm

7. (*c*) Length of each step of Smith = 75 cm

Total number of steps taken by Smith = 20000

$\therefore$ Distance covered in 20000 steps

= (20000 × 75) cm = 1500000 cm = 15 km

Given, 1 mile = 1.6 km

$\Rightarrow \quad 1 \text{ km} = \frac{1}{1.6}$ miles

$\therefore \quad 15 \text{ km} = \left(15 \times \frac{1}{1.6}\right)$ miles = 9.375 miles

8. (*c*) Length of bridge = 600 m

Length of truck = 5 m

Gap between the trucks = 1 m

$\therefore$ Total length required by 1 truck

= Length of a truck + Gap between trucks

= 5 m + 1 m = 6 m

So, number of trucks that can stand on the bridge = 600 m ÷ 6 m = 100 trucks

9. (*b*) Length of gift = 38 cm

Length of wrapping paper = 64 cm

Margin to be left on both sides

= 5 cm + 5 cm = 10 cm

$\therefore$ Length of wrapping paper left

$= 64\text{ cm} - (38\text{ cm} + 10\text{ cm})$

$= 64\text{ cm} - 48\text{ cm} = 16\text{ cm}$

10. (*a*)

I. $8 \times 1000\text{ g} = 8000\text{ g} = 8\text{ kg}$

II. $900\text{ g} + 100\text{ g} = 1000\text{ g} = 1\text{ kg}$

III. $4000\text{ g} \div 4 = 1000\text{ g} = 1\text{ kg}$

IV. $780\text{ g} - 280\text{ g} = 500\text{ g} = 0.5\text{ kg}$

Hence, option (a) is the correct answer.

11. (*a*) Weight on 1st pan = 750 g

Weight on 2nd pan = 2 kg = 2000 g

In order to balance the scales, weight on 1st pan must be equal to the weight on 2nd pan.

$\therefore$ Weight needed to add on 1st pan

$= 2000\text{ g} - 750\text{ g} = 1250\text{ g}$

12. (*b*) Given,

Weight of 3 books + Weight of 1 puppy = 12 kg

According to the given diagram,

Weight of 3 books = Weight of 1 puppy

$\Rightarrow$ Weight of 3 books $= 12\text{ kg} \div 2 = 6\text{ kg}$

[$\because$ there are two elements, i.e., book and puppy]

$\therefore$ Weight of 1 book $= 6\text{ kg} \div 3 = 2\text{ kg}$

13. (*b*) According to the question,

Weight of 2 apples = 20 g

$\Rightarrow$ Weight of 1 apple $= 20\text{ g} \div 2 = 10\text{ g}$

Weight of 2 mangoes and 1 apple = 46 g

$\Rightarrow$ Weight of 2 mangoes $= 46\text{ g} - 10\text{ g} = 36\text{ g}$

$\Rightarrow$ Weight of 1 mango $= 36\text{ g} \div 2 = 18\text{ g}$

and weight of 1 mango and 1 pear = 24 g

$\therefore$ Weight of 1 pear $= 24\text{ g} - 18\text{ g} = 6\text{ g}$

14. (*b*) All options are correct except option (b).

4 L 50 mL = 4050 mL.

Hence, option (b) is incorrect.

15. (*d*) Correct order is II < IV < I < III.

Since, spoon holds lesser quantity than all.

A cup will hold less quantity than kettle and bucket. Kettle holds lesser quantity than bucket finally bucket will hold highest quantity among all.

16. (*c*) All except potatoes are measured in litre or millilitre.

17. (*c*) Volume of lemonade = 400 mL

Volume of lemonade Moishe drank

$= \frac{1}{4}$ of $400\text{ mL} = 100\text{ mL}$

$\therefore$ Volume of lemonade left

= Total volume – Volume drank

$= 400\text{ mL} - 100\text{ mL} = 300\text{ mL}$

18. (*c*) According to the diagram,

Number of patients = 14

Volume of syrup = 1190 mL

$\therefore$ Volume of syrup given to each patient

$= 1190\text{ mL} \div 14 = 85\text{ mL}$

19. (*d*) Volume of water in a tank = 1.5 kL

$= 1.5 \times 1000\text{L} = 1500\text{ L}$

Volume of bucket = 125 L

$\therefore$ Number of buckets required to empty the tank $= 1500\text{ L} \div 125\text{ L} = 12$

20. (*b*) Given,

Total volume of petrol required by Danny excluding Thursday

$= 240\text{ mL} + 560\text{ mL} + 385\text{ mL} + 358\text{ mL} + 237\text{ mL}$

$= 1780\text{ mL} = 1.78\text{ L}$ [$\because 1\text{ L} = 1000\text{ mL}$]

and volume of petrol required in entire week

$= 2180\text{ mL} = 2.18\text{ L}$

$\therefore$ Volume of petrol required on Thursday

$= 2.18\text{ L} - 1.78\text{ L} = 0.40\text{ L} = 400\text{ mL}$

21. (*c*) Considering option (c), Volume of oil in bottles *B* and *D*

$= 1\text{ L } 650\text{ mL} + 2\text{ L } 692\text{ mL}$

$= 1650\text{ mL} + 2692\text{ mL}$

$= 4342\text{ mL} = 4\text{ L } 342\text{ mL}$

Hence, option (c) is the correct answer.

22. (*b*) I. True.

II. False, long distances are measured in kilometre.

III. True.

IV. True.

7. Money

1. *(a)* Given, $\frac{1}{4}$ of ₹ $x = 25$ paise

$\Rightarrow \quad \frac{1}{4} \times ₹\, x = ₹\, \frac{25}{100}$

$\therefore \quad x = ₹\, \frac{25 \times 4}{100} = ₹\, 1$

2. *(b)* Considering all options :

Option (a), (10×50) paise $= ₹\, 5$

[$\because$ 100 paise = ₹ 1]

Option (b), (14×50) paise $= ₹\, 7$

Option (c), (20×50) paise $= ₹\, 10$

Option (d), (24×50) paise $= ₹\, 12$

Hence, option (b) is correct.

3. *(c)* Option (a), 280 paise = ₹ 2.80

[$\because$ ₹ 1 = 100 paise]

Option (b), ₹ 4.85

Option (c), (5×25) paise $= ₹\, 1.25$

Option (d), Twenty 10 paise coins

$= 20 \times 0.10 = ₹\, 2$

So, option (c) has the least value.

4. *(d)* I. ₹ 48 ÷ ₹ 3 = ₹ 16

II. (16×25) paise = 400 paise = ₹ 4

III. ₹ 23.25 − ₹ 6.95 = ₹ 16.30

IV. ₹ 19.65 − 25 paise = ₹ 19.65 − ₹ 0.25

= ₹ 19.40

5. *(d)* I. 560 paise = ₹ 5.60

$\therefore$ ₹ 5.60 < ₹ 7.80

II. $\frac{2}{3}$ of ₹ 9 $= \frac{2}{3} \times$ ₹ 9 = ₹ 6 and 600 paise = ₹ 6

$\therefore$ $\frac{2}{3}$ of ₹ 9 = 600 paise

III. 7 one rupee note $= 7 \times ₹\, 1 = ₹\, 7$

10 fifty paise coins $= ₹\, (10 \times 0.50) = ₹\, 5$

$\therefore$ 7 one rupee note > 10 fifty paise coins.

IV. 6 rupees and 25 paise = ₹ 6.25

5 rupees and 200 paise = ₹ 5 + ₹ 2 = ₹ 7

$\therefore$ 6 rupees and 25 paise < 5 rupees and 200 paise.

6. *(a)* Option (a), $4 \times 2 + 1 \times 1 + 1 \times 0.25$

= ₹ 8 + ₹ 1 + ₹ 0.25 = ₹ 9.25

Option (b), $4 \times 2 + 1 \times 0.50 + 1 \times 0.25$

= ₹ 8 + ₹ 0.50 + ₹ 0.25 = ₹ 8.75

Option (c), $1 \times 5 + 12 \times 0.50$ = ₹ 5 + ₹ 6 = ₹ 11

Option (d), $1 \times 5 + 2 \times 1 + 6 \times 0.25$

= ₹ 5 + ₹ 2 + ₹ 1.5 = ₹ 8.5

Hence, option (a) is the correct answer.

7. *(c)* Option (c), Cost of a bow = ₹ 50

$\Rightarrow$ Cost of two bows = ₹ (2×50) = ₹ 100

Cost of winter cap = ₹ 75

Cost of a purse = ₹ 200

$\therefore$ Total cost of two bows, a winter cap and a purse = ₹ 100 + ₹ 75 + ₹ 200 = ₹ 375

Total money Suzanne has = ₹ 500

So, she can buy two bows, a winter cap and a purse.

Hence , option (c) is the correct answer.

8. *(c)* I. True.

II. False, ₹ 5.75 means five hundred seventy five paise.

III. False, there are 400 twenty five paise coins in ₹ 100.

IV. True, the given amount is equal to ₹ 14.85.

9. *(d)* I. 500 paise makes ₹ <u>5</u>

II. <u>250</u> paise makes two and a half rupee.

III. $\frac{3}{4}$ of ₹ 1 $= \frac{3}{4} \times 100$ paise = <u>75</u> paise.

IV. Cost of 1 cup of tea = ₹ 6

$\therefore$ Cost of 5 cups of tea = ₹ (6×5) = ₹ <u>30</u>

Hence, option (d) is correct.

10. *(b)* Given, money received by Jack = ₹ 200

and 1 Pencil box = ₹ 40

$\therefore$ Number of pencil box = ₹ 200 ÷ 40 = 5

11. (b) Number of hours Christina worked = 15 hours

Money earned in 1 hour = ₹ 100

Money earned in 15 hours

= ₹ (100×15) = ₹ 1500

Money spent $= \frac{1}{4}$ th of ₹ 1500

$= \frac{1}{4} \times$ ₹ 1500 = ₹ 375

$\therefore$ Money left with Christina = ₹1500 − ₹375
= ₹1125

12. (d) According to the question,
Money saved by Hannu in 1st week = ₹20
Money saved by Hannu in 2 weeks = ₹60
(₹20 + ₹40)
Money saved by Hannu in 3 weeks = ₹120
(₹20 + ₹40 + ₹60)
Money saved by Hannu in 4 weeks
= ₹120 + ₹80 = ₹200
Hence, after 4 weeks, Hannu will be able to buy the video game.

13. (a) Savings of Kirti = ₹415
According to the question,
Kirti has four ₹10 notes and twenty five ₹1 notes = 4 × ₹10 + 25 × ₹1 = ₹(40 + 25) = ₹65
$\therefore$ Money left = ₹415 − ₹65 = ₹350
So, number of notes of ₹50 = ₹350 ÷ ₹50 = 7

14. (c) Cost of cricket bat = ₹180
Total money Bunny has = ₹500
$\therefore$ Money left with Bunny
= Total money − Money spent on cricket bat
= ₹500 − ₹180 = ₹320

15. (a) Price of 1 bouquet = ₹50
Number of flowers in 1 bouquet = 10
$\therefore$ Number of bouquet made out of 600 flowers = $\frac{600}{10} = 60$
$\therefore$ Price of 60 bouquet = ₹(50 × 60) = ₹3000

16. (c) Cost of 1 pen = ₹17.75
$\Rightarrow$ Cost of 5 pens = 17.75 × 5 = ₹88.75
Given, money left with Stella = ₹15.95
$\therefore$ Money which Stella had at first
= Money spent + Money left
= ₹88.75 + ₹15.95 = ₹104.70

17. (a) Total cost of 4 toy cars and 6 cookies
= ₹572
According to the question,
Cost of 1 toy car = ₹38 + Cost of 1 cookie
$\Rightarrow$ Cost of 4 toy cars
= 4 × (₹38 + Cost of 1 cookie)
= ₹152 + Cost of 4 cookies
$\therefore$ Cost of 6 cookies + Cost of 4 toy cars
= ₹572
$\Rightarrow$ Cost of 6 cookies + ₹152
+ Cost of 4 cookies
= ₹572
$\Rightarrow$ Cost of 10 cookies = ₹572 − ₹152 = ₹420
$\therefore$ Cost of 1 cookie = ₹420 ÷ 10 = ₹42

18. (d) Tessie had = 15 kg newspaper
Amount Tessie received = ₹(6×15) = ₹90
Adira had = 13 kg plastic
Amount Adira received = ₹(12×13) = ₹156
Tulip had = 2 kg iron and 4 kg brass
= 2 × ₹14 + 4 × ₹180
= ₹28 + ₹720 = ₹748
$\therefore$ Total amount Ragman paid
= ₹748 + ₹156 + ₹90 = ₹994
So, Statement (d) is correct.

19. (d) Price of 1 shirt = ₹125.75
Money I had = ₹754.50
$\therefore$ Number of shirts bought = $\frac{754.50}{125.75} = 6$
Since, one shirt is free with two.
So, I will get 3 shirts more on purchase of 6 shirts.
$\therefore$ Total shirts bought = 6 + 3 = 9

20. (c) Cost of 1 notebook = ₹75
Cost of 5 notebooks = ₹75 × 5 = ₹375
Cost of 1 ruler = ₹5.5
Cost of 2 ruler = ₹5.5 × 2 = ₹11
Cost of 1 pencil = ₹4
Cost of 12 pencils = ₹12 × ₹4 = ₹48
Cost of Geometry box = ₹82
Total bill = 375 + 11 + 48 + 82 = ₹516

8. Time and Calendar

1. (c) Since, the hour hand is between 6 and 7 and minute hand is on 10. So, the clock shows 6 : 50, which is same as 18 : 50.

2. (c) Given time = 3 : 50
Quarter to 5 = 4 : 45
$\therefore$ Required time = 4 : 45 − 3 : 50 = 55 min
After 55 more min, time will be 4 : 45.

3. *(c)* Indian Standard Time = 2 : 55 pm

According to the questions,

Indian Standard Time

= Greenwich Mean Time + 5 h 30 min

∴ Greenwich Mean Time

= Indian Standard Time – 5 h 30 min

= 2 : 55 pm – 5h 30 min = 9 : 25 am

4. *(b)* Time in India = 12 : 53 pm

Time difference = 15 h

∴ Time in USA

= Time in India + Time difference

= 12 : 53 pm + 15 h

= 12 : 53 pm + 12 h + 3 h

= 12 : 53 am + 3 h = 3 : 53 am

5. *(c)* Time when rain started = 10 : 07 am

Time when rain stopped = 3 : 15 pm

∴ Elapsed time/Period of rainfall

= 3 : 15 pm – 10 : 07 am

= 5 h 8 min

6. *(c)* Time of sunrise = 5:52 am

Time of day light hour = 13 h 32 min

∴Time of sunset

= 5 : 52 am + 13 h 32 min = 7 : 24 pm

7. *(a)* Time at which Amelie completed baking the cake = 17 : 35

Time used for baking = 2 h and 15 min

∴Time at which she started baking

= 17 : 35 – 2 h 15 min = 15 : 20

8. *(d)* I. False, 3 h = $3 \times 60 \times 60$ s = 10800 s

and 14 min = 14×60 s = 840 s

∴ 3 h 14 min = 10800 + 840 s = 11640 s

II. False, 5 : 30 pm is same as 17 : 30.

III. False, 3 h 49 min – 2 h 58 min = 51 min

IV. True.

Hence, option (d) is correct

9. *(c)* A = 18 : 30, B = 13 : 20, C = 8 : 50, D = 23 : 55

So, A → 4; B → 3; C → 2; D → 1

10. *(d)* Time at which Jessica arrived = 8 : 12 am

Opening time of nursery on Tuesday = 8 : 30 am

So, Jessica will have to wait

= 8 : 30 am – 8 : 12 am = 18 min.

11. *(a)* Time at the train reached Ajmer station

= 6 : 00 pm

Travelling time = 8 h

Waiting time at Shahdra station = 10 min

Arriving time at station after getting 1 h 15 min late = 6:00 pm

– (8 h + 10 min + 1 h 15 min)

= 8 : 35 am

12. *(c)*

P. 8:30 am in 24-hour clock time is written as 08:30.

Q. 14:00 in 12-hour clock time is written as 2:00 pm.

R. 18:20 in 12-hour clock time is written as 6:20 pm.

S. 2:30 am in 24-hour clock time is written as 02:30.

13. *(b)* Time of leaving from London

= 2 : 20 pm on Tuesday

Time of arriving in Sydney

= 6 : 40 pm on Wednesday

Time difference between London and Sydney

= 11 h

According to the question,

Time of arriving in Sydney as per the London time = 6 : 40 pm Wednesday – 11 h

= 7 : 40 am Wednesday

∴ Duration of flight = 2 : 20 pm Tuesday

– 7 : 40 am Wednesday

= 17 h 20 min

14. *(a)* Day on 1st July = Monday

Number of days in July = 31

∴ Total number of days till 15th August excluding 1st July = 30 + 15 = 45

We know that , 45 = $7 \times 6 + 3$

Since, day repeats after 7 days, so it will be Monday on 12th August,

Tuesday on 13th August,

Wednesday on 14th August

and Thursday on 15th August.

15. *(c)* Since, the year is 2012 and it is divisible by 4, so the year is a leap year.

$\therefore$ Number of days in February = 29

and number of days in 2012 (leap year) = 366

So, required fraction $= \frac{29}{366}$

16. *(d)* According to the question

(i) Kate and Suzanne have their birthdays in the same month, i.e., Kate and Suzanne have birthdays on June 15th and June 21st.

(ii) Julia and Suzanne have their birthdays on the same day of a month, i.e., on February 21st and June 21st.
Hence, Kate, Julia and Suzanne are not born on August 3rd.
So, Helena was born on August 3rd.

17. *(b)* Expiry date of the given product

$= 7/20 =$ July 2020

Manufacturing date of given product

$= 5/19 =$ May 2019

$\therefore$ Elapsed time = 1 yr and 2 months

18. *(a)* According to the question,

Date on which Sally got new phone

= January 15

Number of days in 1 week and 5 days

$= (7 + 5)$ days $= 12$ days

[$\because$ 1 week = 7 days]

Today's date = 15 January + 12 days

= 27th January

19. *(a)* First lesson of Sara

= 15th March, Thursday

Second lesson of Sara = 18th March, Sunday

Third lesson of Sara = 21st March, Wednesday

Fourth lesson of Sara = 24th March, Saturday

Fifth lesson of Sara = 27th March, Tuesday

Sixth lesson of Sara = 30th March, Friday

Hence, Sara will not have any class on Monday.

20. *(d)* As given Calendar, forth Tuesday on her brother's birthday is 26th September.

So, 10th day before from 26th September is 17th September.

Hence, Somya will mark her birthday on 17th September.

9. Lines and Angles

1. *(c)*

(a) Tip of a pencil is an example of a point.

(b) Equator line is an example of a line because it is infinite.

(c) Flashlight is an example of a ray, since it originates from torch/headlight and extends infinitely from the other side.

(d) Edges of paper is an example of a line segment because its length is fixed.
Hence, option (c) is correct.

2. *(c)* Ray has one end point.

3. *(d)* Jiya places arrow at only one end point of the line segment, which means that the line segment can be extended up to infinitely in only one direction. Thus, it is ray.

4. *(a)* The four points together forms a straight line.

5. *(c)* The line joining the three points KGE is parallel to the line *m*.

6. *(d)* Only figure 1 shows the pair of parallel lines. Hence, option (d) is correct.

7. *(c)* Adjacent edges of table top is an example of intersecting lines.

8. *(b)* (i) (B); (ii) (C); (iii) (A)

9. *(d)* $P =$ no

$Q =$ one

$R =$ point of intersection

$S =$ both

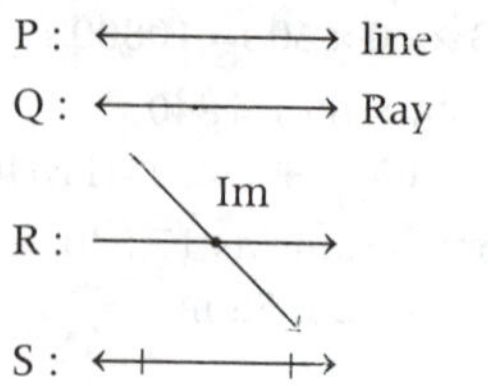

10. *(b)* There are 11 alphabets which are made up of curved lines, i.e., B, C, D, G, J, O, P, Q, R, S, U.

11. *(a)* According to the given figure,

1st line, points P, Q, R and S make a rays in right direction and points S, R, Q and P make a rays in left direction.

So, total number of rays = 4 + 4 = 8

Similarly in IInd line, total number of rays

$= 4 + 4 = 8$

and IIIrd line, total number of rays

$= 4 + 4 = 8$

So, total number of rays in the given figure

$= 8 + 8 + 8 = 24$

Hence, option (a) is correct.

12. *(a)* If we joined all points, we will gets line segments

$\overline{AB}, \overline{BC}, \overline{CD}, \overline{DA}, \overline{AC}, \overline{BD}$

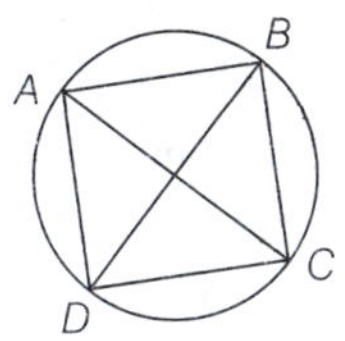

Hence, total number of line segments are 6.

13. *(c)* Line segments in the given figure are

$\overline{AB}, \overline{BC}, \overline{CD}, \overline{DE}, \overline{EF}, \overline{FG}, \overline{GH}, \overline{HI}, \overline{IJ}, \overline{JA}, \overline{OA}, \overline{OB}, \overline{OC}, \overline{OD}, \overline{OE}, \overline{OF}, \overline{OG}, \overline{OH}, \overline{OI}, \overline{OJ}$.

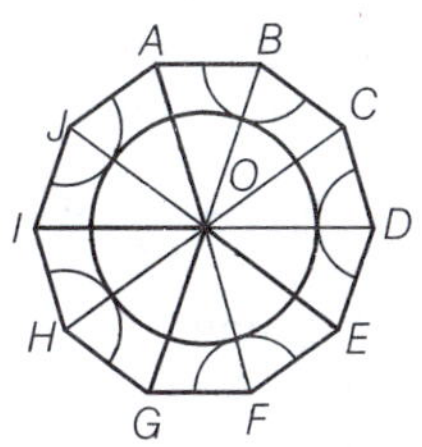

So, there are 20 lines segments.

14. *(a)* Here, the total number of line segments are 10.

$(\overline{AB}, \overline{BF}, \overline{AF}, \overline{BC}, \overline{FE}, \overline{CE}, \overline{CD}, \overline{ED}, \overline{BE}, \overline{CF})$

15. *(a)* The given, $\angle AOB$ is an acute angle.

16. *(a)* We know that, obtuse angle is greater than 90° and 147° is greater than 90°.

So, Rob makes an obtuse angle.

17. *(d)* The given figure consists of two right angles, one acute angle and one obtuse angle.

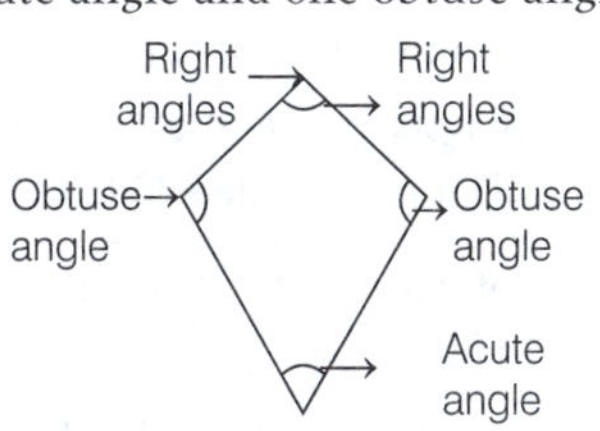

18. *(c)* I. The hands of the first clock are inclined at an angles less than 90°. Hence, they form an acute angle.

II. The hands of the second clock are inclined at an angle greater than 90°.

Hence, they form an obtuse angle.

III. The hands of the third clock are inclined at 90°. Hence, they form a right angle.

19. *(a)* As we know a right angle measures 90°.

$\therefore$ (i) Right.

An acute angle is less than 90°.

$\therefore$ (ii) acute

A straight angle measures equal to two right angles.

$\therefore$ (iii) straight

An obtuse angle is greater than a right angle and less than a straight angle.

$\therefore$ (iv) right

20. *(b)* There are 15 angles in the given figure.

$\angle ABC$, $\angle BCA$, $\angle BAC$, $\angle APQ$, $\angle AQP$, $\angle BPQ$, $\angle CQP$, $\angle ARS$, $\angle ASR$, $\angle BRS$, $\angle CSR$, $\angle AEF$, $\angle AFE$, $\angle BEF$ and $\angle CFE$.

10. Area and Perimeter

1. *(c)* Perimeter of ΔPQR

$= PQ + QR + RP$

[$\because$ perimeter of triangle = sum of all sides]

$= 5\text{ cm} + 3\text{ cm} + 7.8\text{ cm} = 15.8\text{ cm}$

2. *(c)* Given, breadth of the cut-out figure is 1/3rd the breadth of sheet.

$\Rightarrow$ Breadth of cut-out figure $= \frac{1}{3} \times 6 = 2\text{ m}$

and it can be seen from the diagram that length of the cut-out figure $= 12 \div 2 = 6\text{ m}$

$\therefore$ Perimeter of cut-out figure

$= 2 \times (\text{Length} + \text{Breadth})$

$= 2 \times (6 + 2) = 16\text{ m}$

3. *(b)* Here, boundary of garden A

$= 2 \times (\text{Length} + \text{Breadth})$

$= 2 \times (12 + 8) = 2 \times 20 = 40\text{ m}$

Boundary of garden $B = 2 \times (14 + 12)$
$= 2 \times 26 = 52$ m
Boundary of garden $C = 2 \times (10 + 8)$
$= 2 \times 18 = 36$ m
Boundary of garden $D = 2 \times (14 + 5)$
$= 2 \times 19 = 38$ m
So, garden B has largest boundary.

4. (c) From the above calculation, it is clear that garden C has smallest boundary.
If breadth of garden C is increased by 4 m
$= 8 + 4 = 12$ m
Then, perimeter $= 2 \times (10 + 12) = 44$ m
Hence, ascending order : Garden D < Garden A < Garden C < Garden B
So, garden C is in the third position.

5. (a) Perimeter = Sum of lengths of all sides
$= AB + BC + CD + DE + EF + FA$
$= [3.1 + 3.4 + 3.8 + 3.7 + (3.1 + 3.8) + (3.4 + 3.7)]$ cm $= 28$ cm

6. (c) Given, side of figure 1 = 8 cm.
$\Rightarrow$ Perimeter of figure 1
$= 8 + 8 + 8 + 8 + 8 = 40$ cm
[$\because$ all sides are equal]
Given,
Perimeter of figure 1 = Perimeter of figure 2
Number of sides figure 2 has = 8
Perimeter of figure 2 = 40 cm
$\therefore$ Length of each side $= 40 \div 8 = 5$ cm

7. (b) Distance covered by Ishika in 1 complete round
$= AB + BC + CD + DE + EF + FA$
$= 60 + 30 + 50 + 40 + 110 + 70$
$= 360$ m
$\therefore$ Distance covered by Ishika in 5 complete round
= Distance covered in 1 round × 5
$= 360 \times 5 = 1800$ m

8. (a) Perimeter of figure (i) $= (20 + 1 + 20 + 1)$ cm
$= 42$ cm
Perimeter of figure (ii) $= (20 + 2 + 20 + 2)$ cm
$= 44$ cm
$\therefore$ Required difference $= (44 - 42)$ cm $= 2$ cm

9. (c) Perimeter = Sum of all sides = 28 units.
When the left out square is placed at C, the perimeter will get reduced by 4 units. Since, the position of C square bounded by all four sides.

10. (a) Field is in the shape of a square whose side is 24 m.
$\therefore$ Area in which the cow can graze
= Side × Side
$= (24 \times 24)\ m^2 = 576\ m^2$

11. (c) Given, length = 12 cm and breadth = 10 cm
$\therefore$ Area of rectangle = Length × Breadth
$= 12 \times 10 = 120\ cm^2$
So, area of each piece $= 120 \div 4 = 30\ cm^2$

12. (d) Area of the given figure as follows :
a = 12 sq. units
r = 7 sq. units
E = 10 sq. units
a = 12 sq. units
$\therefore$ Total area $= (12 + 7 + 10 + 12)$ sq. units
$= 41$ sq. units

13. (a) On counting number of squares, we got the area of
Figure A = 7 sq. units
Figure B = 10 sq. units
Figure C = 16 sq. units
Figure D = 20 sq. units
So, smallest area occupied by figure (A).

14. (c) From the above calculation, figure B and figure C have a total area of 26 sq. units.
i.e., Total area = Area of figure B + Area of figure C
$= 10 + 16 = 26$ sq. units.
Hence, option (c) is correct.

15. (c) Given, radius of circle = 3 cm
Then, diameter of circle $= (2 \times 3)$ cm $= 6$ cm
$\Rightarrow$ Side of square = Diameter of circle = 6 cm
$\therefore$ Area of square = Side × Side $= 6 \times 6 = 36\ cm^2$

16. (a) Area of backyard = 20 sq. ft
Length of basketball court = 5 ft
Breadth of basketball court = 4 ft

∴ Area of basketball court

$= (5 \times 4)$ sq. ft $= 20$ sq. ft

So, area of backyard is equal to area of basketball court.

17. (*d*) Length of park $= 65$ m

Breadth of park $= 52$ m

∴ Area of park = Length × Breadth

$= (65 \times 52)\, m^2 = 3380\, m^2$

Area occupied by each girl

$= 3380 \div 5 = 676\, m^2$

∴ Area occupied by remaining 3 girls

$= 676 \times 3 = 2028\, m^2$

18. (*a*) Area of figure A $= 40 \times 40 = 1600\, cm^2$

∴ Area of figure B = area of figure A – 5 square of side 10 cm

$= 1600 - 5 \times (10 \times 10)$

$= 1600 - (5 \times 100)$

$= 1600 - 500 = 1100\, cm^2$

∴ Difference between the area of figure A and figure B

= Area of figure A – Area of figure B

$= 1600 - 1100 = 500\, cm^2$

19. (*d*) Given, length of wall $= 28$ m

And breadth of wall $= 21$ m

∴ Area of wall = Length × Breadth

$= 28 \times 21 = 588\, m^2$

Area of wall painted green $= \frac{1}{3} \times 588 = 196\, m^2$

Remaining area $= (588 - 196)\, m^2 = 392\, m^2$

So, area painted blue $= (392 \div 2)\, m^2 = 196\, m^2$

∴ Remaining area which is to be painted

$= (392 - 196)\, m^2 = 196\, m^2$

20. (*a*) Perimeter of 1st square $= 40$ cm

Perimeter of 2nd square $= 32$ cm

Perimeter of 3rd square = Perimeter of 1st square – Perimeter of 2nd square

$= (40 - 32)$ cm $= 8$ cm

Since, perimeter of square $= 4 \times$ Side

⇒ Side of square = Perimeter ÷ 4

$= (8 \div 4)$ cm $= 2$ cm

21. (*b*) Length of path $= 40$ m

breadth of path $= 5$ m

∴ Area of path $= 40 \times 5 = 200\, m^2$

∴ Length of garden $= 40$ m

breath of garden $= 25$ m

Area of garden $= 40 \times 25 = 1000\, m^2$

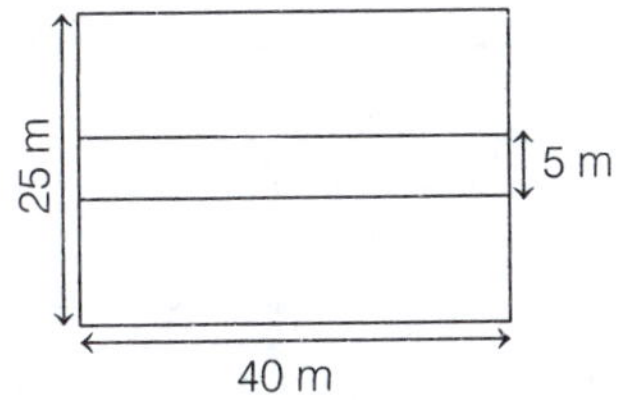

∴ Area of garden excluding path

$= 1000 - 200 = 800\, m^2$

22. (*a*) Both Rahul and Rosy have same starting and Rahul runs faster than Rosy yet he loses the race, because perimeter of outer circle or track is more than the perimeter of inner circle or track.

Hence, option (a) is correct.

23. (*c*) I. Perimeter is expressed in units of length.

II. Perimeter of a triangle with sides a, b and c is $a + b + c$.

III. Perimeter of a regular hexagon is $6 \times$ sides.

IV. Area of 15 unit squares is 15 sq units.

11. Pattern and Symmetry

1. (*d*) Let A = ◯, B = ▯, C = ☆, D = ⬡

Then, given pattern is as follows :

ABCD ABCD [AB]

So, ◯ ▯ will be the next two shapes.

Hence, options d is correct.

2. (*a*) Cyra is standing upright in every odd number of turns and upside down in every even number of turns, i.e., in Ist turn, Cyra is standing upright and in IInd turn, Cyra is upside down and so on.

So, in 13th turn Cyra will be standing up right because 13 is an odd number.

3. *(c)* Here, in first figure, top circle is shaded, in second figure, triangle is shaded and in third figure, bottom two circles are shaded and the pattern will continues

i.e.,

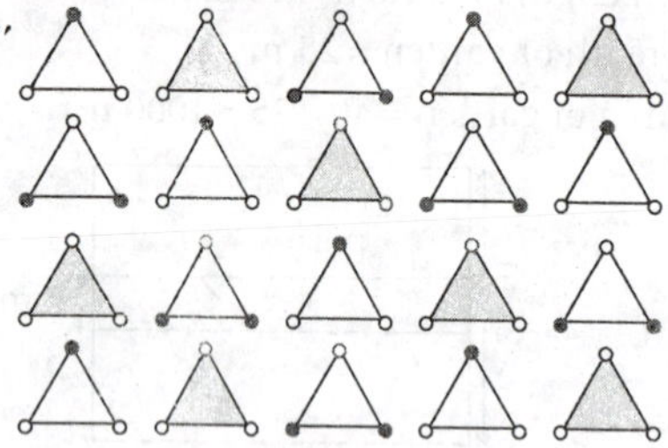

So, the number of figures with shaded triangles
$= 7$

4. *(b)* Here, in every step, number of squares is equal to the number of steps.

Hence, in 5th step, there will be 5 squares with the arrangement as in option (b).

5. *(a)* Here, in the given pattern from first figure to second figure one side is reduced. Similarly, second figure to third figure one side is reduced and so on.

So, figure in option (a), will be the next figure in the given pattern.

Hence, option (a) is correct.

6. *(b)* Here, in each option except (b), the number of sides in outer shape is one more than the number of sides in inner shape.

7. *(a)* Here, in every option except (a), number of semi-circle is 6.

Number of Semi-circle in option (a) is 7.

8. *(d)* Here, the figure must fit in the given pattern. Only, option (d) fits completely.

9. *(c)* Here, the letter E is taking $\frac{1}{4}$ th turn in every step in anti-clockwise direction.

So, next shape will be E.

Hence, option (c) is correct.

10. *(a)* Here, the dot inside circle is rotating in clockwise direction and the dot outside the circle is rotating in anti-clockwise direction.

Hence, option (a) is the correct answer.

11. *(a)* Here, the pattern is as follows:

Number in Ist column
$\times$ Number in IInd column
$=$ Number in IIIrd column

i.e., In Ist row, $9 \times 4 = 36$

In IIIrd row, $12 \times 7 = 84$

Similarly, In Ind row, $5 \times A = 60$

$\therefore$ $A = \boxed{12}$

12. *(a)* Here, in each number 13 is added to get the next number.

i.e.,
$$39 + 13 = 52$$
$$52 + 13 = 65$$
$$65 + 13 = \boxed{78} = A$$
$$78 + 13 = 91$$
$$91 + 13 = \boxed{104} = B$$

$\therefore$ $B - A = 104 - 78 = 26$

13. *(c)* Here, the previous terms are added to get the next term.

i.e., $0 + 1 = 1$; $1 + 1 = 2$; $1 + 2 = 3$ and so on.

Hence, option (c) is correct.

14. *(d)* Here, the pattern is as follows :
$$10000 - 800 = 9200$$
$$9200 - 800 = 8400$$
$$8400 - 800 = 7600$$

So, none of the numbers is incorrect.

15. *(a)* Only figure option (a) is a symmetric figure.

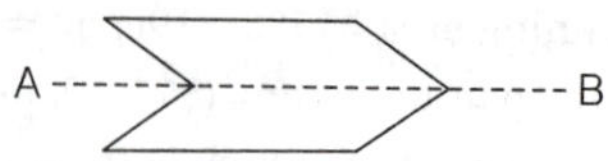

Hence, option (a) is correct.

16. *(d)* Option (a) Option (b)

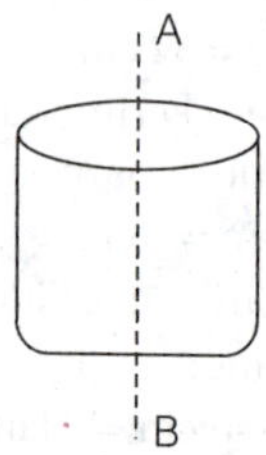

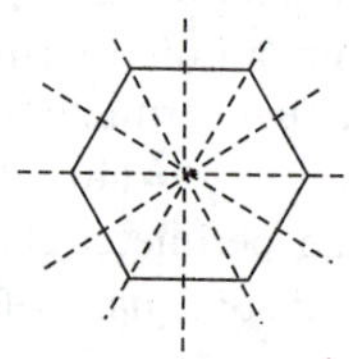

Option (c)

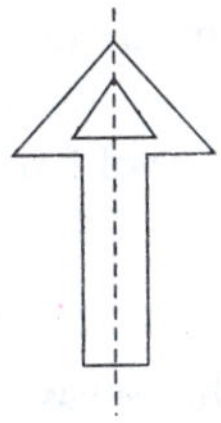

So, only option (d) has no line of symmetry.

17. *(a)*

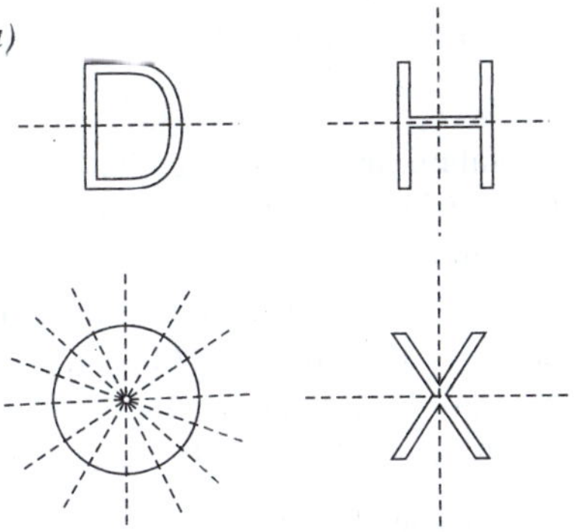

Only letter D has exactly one line of symmetry.
Hence, option (a) is correct.

18. *(a)*

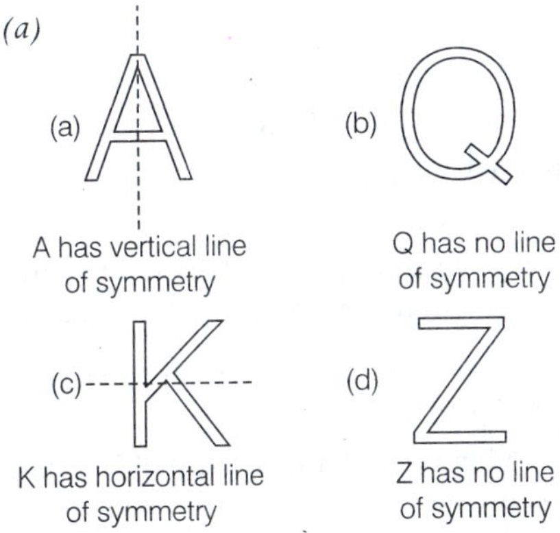

Only letter *A* has vertical line of symmetry.
Hence, option (a) is correct.

19. *(b)*

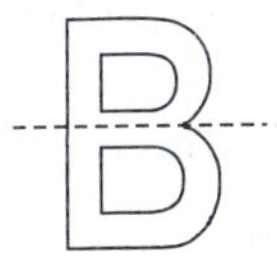

Number of line of symmetry for above figure is 1.

Hence, option (b) is correct.

20. *(a)*

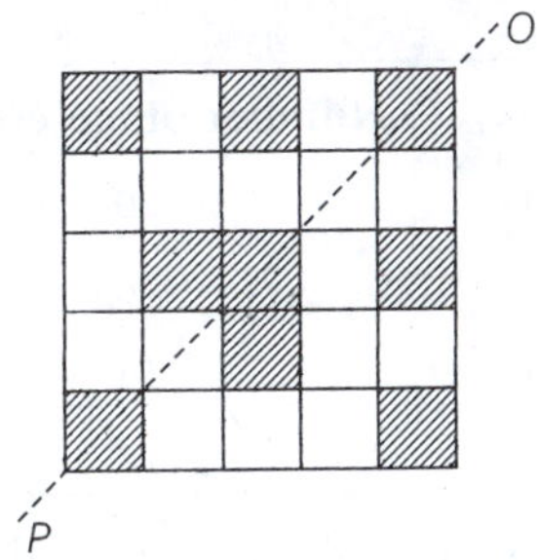

Minimum number of squares that must be shaded is 3.
Hence, option (a) is correct.

12. Data Handling

1. *(b)* Rent = □□ = 1000 + 1000 = ₹ 2000
Food = □□□□ = 1000 + 1000 + 1000 + 1000
= ₹ 4000
Transport = □ = ₹ 1000
Others = □□□ = 1000 + 1000 + 1000
= ₹ 3000
So, family spends the most on food.

2. *(a)* From the given information,
There are 2  in Thursday.
Thus, $2 \times 10 = 20$ students were present on Thursday.
Hence, option (a) is correct.

3. *(b)* From the given information,

City A planted 6  $= 6 \times 500 = 3000$

City B planted 10  $= 10 \times 500 = 5000$

City C planted 7  $= 7 \times 500 = 3500$

City D planted 5  $= 5 \times 500 = 2500$

City E planted 2  $= 2 \times 500 = 1000$

Hence, City B planted maximum number of trees.

4. (c)

Day	Number of ice-creams
1st	20
2nd	16
3rd	14
4th	18

From the above data, it is clear that on 3rd day, 14 ice-creams were sold.

5. (d) From the data (in Q. No. 4), it is clear that on days 1 and 2, total of 36 ice-creams were sold.

6. (a) There are three students who like apples.
Tally mark for 3 is III.
Hence, option (a is correct.

7. (d) A. We can see from the given chart that,
Number of students who like pineapple is 4 and tally mark for 4 is IIII.
∴The given statement is true.

B. From the given chart, we can see Grapes is the least favourite.
∴The given statement is false.

C. from the chart, we can see,
Number of students who like pineapple is 4.
Number of students who like apple is 3.
∴Number of students who like pineapple is more than the number of students who like apple.
∴The given statement is True.

8. (b) According to survey done by Natasha, number of rainy days in different months are

January = 5 days
February = 2 days
March = 4 days
April = 7 days
May = 13 days
June = 15 days

We can see clearly that June has most rainy days.

9. (b) The highest point scored is 10 by green team and hence 9 is the second highest points scored by team blue.

10. (c) Since, marks of Krista is neither increasing constantly nor decreasing.
So, the performance of Krista cannot be determined.

11. (c) Total number of houses = 30
Total number of houses with dog, cat, tortoise and parrot as their pet
$= 12 + 7 + 1 + 5 = 25$
∴ Number of houses with rabbit as their pet
$= 30 - 25 = 5$

12. (c) Total number of children having their birthdays in July, August and September = 14
As per information,
No children have birthday in July and 4 children have birthday in August.
∴ Number of children having their birthdays in September $= 14 - 4 = 10$

13. (c) Total sale of books
$= 200 + 150 + 300 + 250$
$= 900$

14. (d) As per given data,
Maths Olympiad = 12
Science Olympiad = 8
English Olympiad = 6
Computer Olympiad = 14
It is clear that most of the students are interested in Computer Olympiad, i.e., 14.

15. (c) Number of students interested in Maths Olympiad = 12
Number of students interested in English Olympiad = 6
∴ Required difference $= 12 - 6 = 6$

16. (d) The given bar graph shows marks obtained by a student in four subjects in the session of 2014-15.
Hence, option (d) is correct.

17. (d) The student scored second highest marks in Science, i.e., 50.
Since, marks in English = 40
marks in Hindi = 30
marks in Maths = 60
marks in Science = 50

18. *(b)* Marks scored in English = 40

and $\frac{3}{4}$ of 40 = 30 = Marks scored in Hindi

Hence, in Hindi marks is $\frac{3}{4}$ of marks in English.

19. *(b)* Considering option (b),

From the given bar graph,

Number of students having pet animals in class 2 = 100

Number of students having pet animals in class 4 = 60

$\therefore$ Required difference = 100 − 60 = 40

So, the given statement is correct.

Hence, option (b) is correct.

20. *(b)* From the given pie chart, it is clear that

Half of the customers like fries.

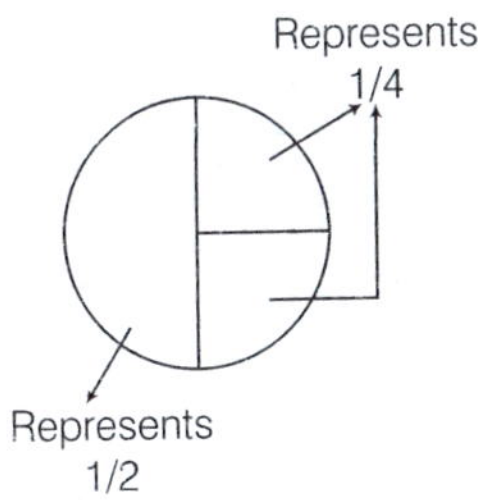

One-fourth of the customers like burger.

One-fourth of the customers like cold coffee.

Hence, option (b) is true.

21. *(c)* From a total of 28 children, 14 are acting which is half of 28 ($28 \div 2 = 14$).

7 are collecting dresses, which is one-fourth of 28 ($28 \div 4 = 7$).

and again 7 are making sets which is one-fourth of 28 ($28 \div 4 = 7$).

$\therefore$ Appropriate pie chart will be

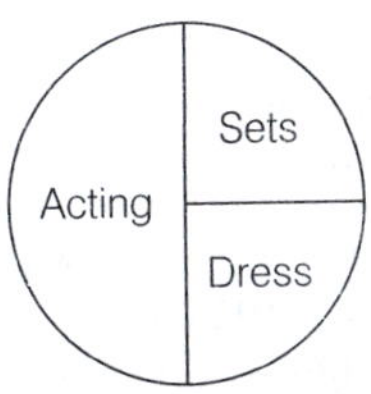

Practice Set 1

1. *(c)* According to the question,

$$78456 \times P = 2589048$$

$$\Rightarrow \quad P = \frac{2589048}{78456} = \frac{78456 \times 33}{78456} = 33$$

2. *(a)* The place value of 3 in number 27345 = 300

And the face value of 3 in number 27345 = 3

$\therefore$ Required product = $300 \times 3 = 900$

3. *(b)* In the given figure 6 parts are shaded out of 12 parts.

$\therefore$ Fraction of shaded part

$$= \frac{\text{Number of shaded parts}}{\text{Total number of parts}} = \frac{6}{12}$$

4. *(d)* According to the given information, the correct name is angle.

5. *(b)*

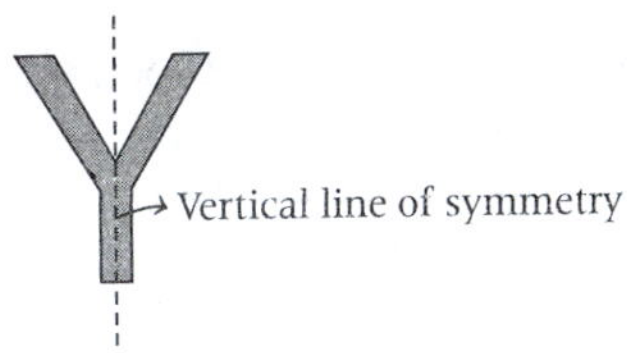

Hence, the option (b) is correct.

6. *(d)* According to the question,

$$x - 2 + 6 + 3 = 12$$

$$\Rightarrow \quad x - 2 + 9 = 12$$

$$\Rightarrow \quad x + 7 = 12$$

$$\Rightarrow \quad x = 12 - 7$$

$$\therefore \quad x = 5$$

7. *(c)* Area is calculated by adding the total number of squares in a figure.

i.e., Area of figure $A \approx 9\text{ cm}^2$

Area of figure $B \approx 10\text{ cm}^2$

Area of figure $C \approx 20\text{ cm}^2$

Area of figure $D \approx 16\text{ cm}^2$

So, figure C occupies the largest area.

8. (*c*) Given time = 5 : 20 pm
Colour of light = red
Number of minutes traffic light stopped working = 25 minutes
Number of minutes traffic light takes to change its colour = 2 minutes
$\therefore$ Light will become green after
= (25 + 2 + 2) minutes = 29 minutes
So, light will be green at
5 : 20 pm + 29 minutes = 5 : 49 pm.

9. (*b*) Weight of box P + Weight of box Q = Weight of box R + Weight of box S

$\Rightarrow \frac{3}{8}$ kg + Weight of box $Q = \left(\frac{1}{4}+\frac{1}{2}\right)$ kg $= \frac{3}{4}$ kg

$\Rightarrow$ Weight of box $Q = \left(\frac{3}{4}-\frac{3}{8}\right)$ kg

$= \left(\frac{6-3}{8}\right)$ kg

$= \frac{3}{8}$ kg

10. (*a*) In figure A, 8 = 2 × 2 × 2 and not 2 × 2.
In figure B, 4 = 2 × 2 and not 3 × 2.
In figure D, 24 = 4 × 6 and not 6 × 6.
So, only figure C, shows the correct factor tree of 24.

11. (*d*) Charge for first kilometre = ₹ 8
Charge for the successive kilometre = ₹10
Distance travelled by Avinash = 58 km
$\therefore$Total money Avinash had to pay
= ₹ 8×1 + ₹10×58 = ₹ 588

12. (*d*)

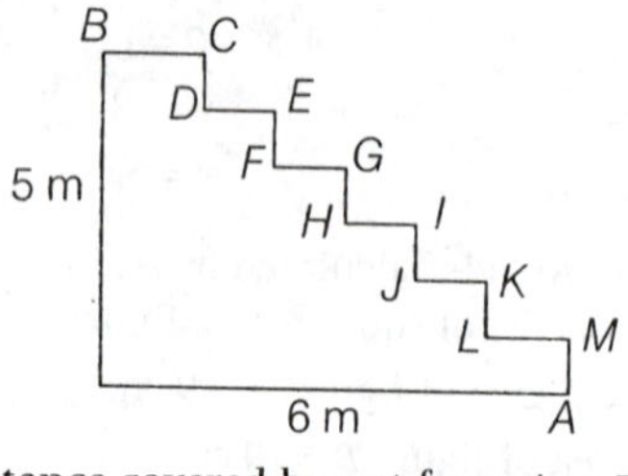

The distance covered by ant from A to B is as follows

$AM + ML + LK + KJ + JI + IH + HG + GF + FE + ED + DC + CB$

$AM + LK + JI + HG + FE + DC = 5$ m

and $BC + DE + FG + HI + JK + LM = 6$ m

$\therefore$ The ant crawls = (5 + 6) = 11 m

13. (*c*) A. Greatest 3-digit number + 1 = 999 + 1
$\Rightarrow$ 1000 = M
B. 12 crore − 15 lakh
= 120000000 − 1500000
= 118500000 = 1185 lakh
C. 135 hundred + 5 hundred
= 13500 + 500 = 14000 = 14 thousand
D. CXXXV + CXLII = 135 + 142 = 277
= CCLXXVII

So, A → (3); B → (1); C → (4); D → (2)

14. (*a*) Given, total number of rows = 428
And total number of seats in each row = 190
$\therefore$Total number of seats = 428 × 190 = 81320

15. (*a*) Total cost of a paper clip, hockey stick and a book = 25 + 155 + 86 = 266
= 100 + 100 + 50 + 10 + 6 = CCLXVI

16. (*a*) Triangles formed are
A, B, C, D, E, F, G, H, EF, HG, FG, EH.

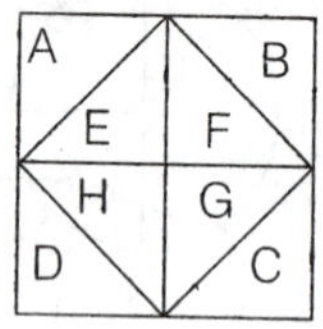

Hence, there are 12 Triangles are there in figure given in question.

17. (*b*) Time at which Krista and her friends started planting = 5 : 00 pm
Time required to plant one sapling = 30 minutes
Number of plants planted on Tuesday = 6
$\therefore$Time required to plant 6 saplings
= 6 × 30 = 180 minutes = 3 hours
So, Krista and her friends get their work done at (5 + 3) = 8 : 00 pm.

18. (*c*) Fine for 1st day = ₹ 1
Fine for 2nd day = ₹ 1
Fine for 3rd day = ₹ 2
Fine for 4th day = ₹ 3
$\therefore$Total fine for 4 days = 3 + 2 + 1 + 1 = ₹ 7

19. (*a*) Given, cost of the book
= ₹192.65
$\therefore$ Fine that library charges = 2 × Cost of book
= 2 × ₹192.65
= ₹ 385.30

20. (*d*) There are 22 line segments in the figure.
$\overline{AC}, \overline{GC}, \overline{AB}, \overline{BC}, \overline{CD}, \overline{DE}, \overline{EB}, \overline{EC}, \overline{DG}, \overline{FG}, \overline{FA}, \overline{FE}, \overline{FC}, \overline{AH}, \overline{BH}, \overline{HC}, \overline{GI}, \overline{DI}, \overline{IC}, \overline{FJ}, \overline{EJ}$ and $\overline{JC}$.

21. (*d*) Here, 6 is subtracted from the numbers in the lower half to get the numbers in the upper half.
i.e., $11 - 6 = 5; 12 - 6 = 6$
Similarly, $25 - 6 = \boxed{19}$
Hence, option (d) is the correct answer.

22. (*c*) Distance travelled on Ist day $= 5\frac{1}{2}$ km
$= \frac{11}{2}$ km
Total distance travelled on both days $= 18$ km
So, distance travelled on 2nd day
$= \left(18 - \frac{11}{2}\right)$ km
$= \left(18 \times \frac{2}{2} - \frac{11}{2}\right)$ km $= \left(\frac{36 - 11}{2}\right)$ km
$= \frac{25}{2}$ km $= 12\frac{1}{2}$ km

23. (*c*) Car *A* will finish the race in $= \frac{3}{4}$
$= 0.75$ minute.
Car *B* will finish the race in $= \frac{7}{11} = 0.63$ min
Car *C* will finish the race in $= \frac{7}{9} = 0.77$ min
Car *D* will finish the race in $= \frac{5}{7} = 0.71$ min
$\because\ 0.63 < 0.71 < 0.75 < 0.77$
$\therefore\ B < D < A < C$
So, option (c) is the correct answer.

24. (*d*) As given in the calendar, 17th May is Saturday and there are 31 days in the month of May. Thus, next two Saturday will be on 24th and 31 st May.
So, last Saturday will be on 31st May.
According to the given information, David went to UK after six days from 31st May.
So, David went to UK on 6th June, 2008.

25. (*a*) Total money earn in a week = ₹ 721
Then, total money earn in 1 day = $721 \div 7$
= ₹103
∴Total money earn in 16 days = ₹103 × 16
= ₹1648

26. (*a*) Observe the ones and tens place of 320 which is 20.
Since, $20 < 50$
∴ 320 will be rounded to previous hundred.
Hence, 320 when rounded off to nearest hundred is 300.

27. (*c*) In order to share pencils equally among three students, the number should be a multiple of 3.
Prashant has 13 pencils ; 13 is not a multiple of 3.
Radhika has 12 pencils ;
$3 \times 4 = 12$ (12 is a multiple of 3)
Sonal has 19 pencils ; 19 is not a multiple of 3.
Neha has 15 pencils ;
$3 \times 5 = 15$ (15 is a multiple of 3)
Hence, Radhika and Neha can share pencils equally among three students.

28. (*a*) Total money spend by Anuj on Friday
= 3.5  = 3.5 × 20 = ₹ 70
Total money spend by Anuj on Thursday
= 2  = 2 × 20 = ₹ 40
∴Required difference = 70 – 40 = ₹ 30

29. (*d*) There are 1 line and 4 rays present in the given figure.

30. (*b*) In the given pattern the circle moves to the next corner in anti-clockwise direction and alternatively it is shaded.
So, figure in option (b) will be the next figure in the given pattern.
Hence, option (b) is correct.

31. (*b*) Capacity of 1 small container = 400 mL
Capacity of 9 small containers
= 400 × 9 = 3600 mL
Capacity of 1 big container = 1500 mL
Capacity of 2 big containers = 1500 × 2 = 3000 mL
So, capacity of the tank = Total capacity of 9 small and 2 big containers = 3600 mL + 3000 mL = 6600 mL = 6 L 600 mL

32. (*d*) Time taken by the wheel in going from one month to next month = 2 seconds
∴ Number of months covered in 30 seconds
$= \frac{30}{2} = 15$
So, starting from April and going anti-clockwise, 15th month will be January.
Hence, wheel will stop on January.

33. (*d*) We have,

$$3 ✿ = 6$$
$$\Rightarrow \quad 1 ✿ = 6 \div 3 = 2$$
$$2\triangle + 1 ✿ = 8$$
$$\Rightarrow \quad 2\triangle = 8 - 2 = 6$$
$$\Rightarrow \quad 1\triangle = 6 \div 2 = 3$$
$$2\square = 28$$
$$\Rightarrow \quad 1\square = 28 \div 2 = 14$$
$$4\bigcirc = 64$$
$$\Rightarrow \quad 1\bigcirc = 64 \div 4 = 16$$
$$\therefore \quad 2 ✿ + 3\triangle + 1\bigcirc + 1\square$$
$$= 2 \times 2 + 3 \times 3 + 1 \times 16 + 1 \times 14$$
$$= 4 + 9 + 16 + 14 = 43$$

34. (*b*) I. False, area is expressed in square units.

II. False, area is measured in square units, while perimeter in measured in units only.

III. False, triangle is a three sided polygon, while quadrilateral is a four sided polygon.

IV. True.

35. (*a*) Total number of girls $= 120$

Number of girls who like music and dance

$$= \frac{1}{3} \text{ of } 120 = \frac{1}{3} \times 120 = 40$$

Given, number of girls who like music $= 14$

So, number of girls who like dance

$$= 40 - 14 = 26.$$

Practice Set 2

1. (*d*) Given, population of city $= 145526$

Since, $5526 > 5000$

$\therefore$ 145526 when rounded off to nearest thousand will become 146000.

2. (*c*) From the given numbers, when 18 is multiplied by 19, the product is 342.

i.e., $18 \times 19 = 342$

3. (*c*) We have ,

(a) $\frac{1 \times 4}{6 \times 4} = \frac{4}{24}$ (b) $\frac{1 \times 3}{8 \times 3} = \frac{3}{24}$

(c) $\frac{2 \times 6}{4 \times 6} = \frac{12}{24}$ (d) $\frac{1}{24}$

Since, it is given that Tancy studied for more number of hours on Tuesday than on Monday.

Among the given options, only (c) represents hours more than 6.

$\therefore$ Tancy studied for 12 hours on Tuesday out of 24 hours.

4. (*d*) $\frac{3}{4} < \frac{9}{10}$ because $\frac{3}{4}$ is less than $\frac{4}{5}$ and $\frac{9}{10}$ is greater than $\frac{4}{5}$.

5. (*b*) Since, $0.42 = \frac{42}{100}$

So, Mia read 42 pages out of 100.

6. (*c*) Since, 4.5 kg $= 4500$ g

and 4500 g $\div$ 300 g $= 15$

$\therefore$ Fifteen 300 g of sugar packets are required to make 4.5 kg.

7. (*b*) Angle is formed by two rays or two line segments with a common end points.

8. (*b*) From the figure it is clear that, the container has $2\frac{1}{5}$ cup of juice.

9. (*c*) Here, Area of rectangle A

$= \text{Length} \times \text{Breadth} = 8.5 \times 2 = 17$ sq cm

Perimeter of rectangle A

$= 2 \times (\text{Length} + \text{Breadth})$

$= 2 \times (8.5 + 2) = 2 \times 10.5 = 21$ cm

Similarly, Area of rectangle $B = 20$ sq cm

Perimeter of rectangle $B = 18$ cm

and since square is also a rectangle.

$\therefore$ Area of rectangle $C = 16$ sq cm

and perimeter of rectangle $C = 16$ cm

$\therefore$ Perimeter of rectangle $A >$ Area of rectangle A and Perimeter of rectangle $C =$ Area of rectangle C

10. (*c*) Since, George wants to distribute 30 pencils and 20 pens among maximum number of children.

Then, we will find the HCF of 30 and 20.

$$30 = 2 \times 3 \times 5$$
$$20 = 2 \times 2 \times 5$$

$\therefore$ HCF (30, 20) $= 10$

So, 30 pencils and 20 pens can be divided equally among 10 children.

Thus, each child will have 3 pencils $(30 \div 10)$ and 2 pens $(20 \div 10)$.

Cost of 3 pencils $= 5 \times 3 =$ ₹15

Cost of 2 pens $= 2 \times 10 =$ ₹ 20

Hence, a child have to pay (₹ 20 + ₹ 15)
= ₹ 35 to Greoge.

11. (a) The letters that cannot be folded into halves are F, G, J, L, N, P, Q, R, S, Z, i.e., 10.

12. (b)

Toppings	Number of votes
Cheese	3
Pepperoni	6
Sausage	4
Mushroom	0
Onion	2

From the above data, it is clear that Sausage is the group's second favourite type of pizza.

13. (a) Total money in piggy bank I = ₹ 34.5
Total money in piggy bank II = ₹ 80
∴ Total money in both piggy banks
= ₹ 80 + ₹ 34.5 = ₹ 114.5
Since, $4 < 5$
So, total money in both piggy banks rounded off to nearest ten is ₹ 110.

14. (c) From the graph, it is clear that there were 160 spectators at the boxing event.

15. (d) Maximum number of spectators are in swimming = 200
Minimum number of spectators are in weight lifting = 80
So, required difference = $200 - 80 = 120$

16. (c) Number of pieces of candy which could be in Louisa's bag = LCM (2, 3, 5) = 30

17. (c) Number of scoops required by each child = 2
Total number of children = 18
Number of scoops in one container = 6
Since, $6 \div 2 = 3$
⇒ Each container can serve 3 children.
∴ Number of containers required = $18 \div 3 = 6$

18. (d) The maximum number which Anouk can get on his both dice is 6.
As, $6 + 6 = 12$
So, Anouk can move a maximum of 12 squares by throwing both the dice once.

19. (b) From the clues, we have that multiples of 5 which are less than 27 are 5, 10, 15, 20, 25.
But the number should be even. So, we have the choice between 10 and 20.
Also, the number should be a factor of 10.
So, 10 is the required number.

20. (c) Here, we have the following number of obtuse angles from each figure
(a) Number of obtuse angles = 3
(b) Number of obtuse angles = 0
(c) Number of obtuse angles = 8
(d) Number of obtuse angles = 6
Hence, option (c) has maximum number of obtuse angles.

21. (b) If the HCF of first two multiples of a number is one of the numbers, then their LCM is the other number.
For example, HCF of first two multiples of 6, i.e. 6 and 12 is 6 and their LCM is 12.

22. (b) Length of the chart paper = 13 cm
Breadth of the chart paper = 8 cm
∴ Area of the chart paper
= Length × Breadth = $13 \times 8 = 104$ cm^2
Area occupied by each stamp = 2 cm^2
∴ Number of stamps that could be placed in the chart paper = $104 \div 2 = 52$

23. (d)

1.25	3.98	4.84	6.53
+ 2.95	× 4	÷ 2	− 1.64
4.2	15.92	2.42	4.89

Arranging in decreasing order, we get
$15.92 < 4.89 < 4.2 < 2.42$
T A M E

24. (c) Given, $(8 \times 2) \times 5 = 16 \times 5 = 80$
From option (c), $8 \times (2 \times 5) = 8 \times 10 = 80$

25. (a) Given,
Number of words in first line = 7
Number of words in second line = 12
Number of words in third line = 17
and so on.
∴ The pattern is
2nd line → 7 + 5 = 12
3rd line → 12 + 5 = 17
4th line → 17 + 5 = 22
5th line → 22 + 5 = 27
6th line → 27 + 5 = 32
7th line → 32 + 5 = 37
8th line → 37 + 5 = 42
So, there will be 42 words in the eighth line.

26. (c) Number of classes from 15th April till 19th June excluding Sunday
= $(16 + 31 + 19) - 9 = 66 - 9 = 57$
Fees of one hour = ₹ 150
∴ Total fees = ₹ 150 × 57 = ₹ 8550

27. *(c)* Here, the numbers on the corners add upto 17 and the numbers in the middle also add upto 17.

i.e., $4+7+3+3=17$ and $3+6+?+5=17$

$\Rightarrow \quad 14+?=17 \quad \therefore \quad ?=17-14=3$

28. *(a)* Figure (a) shows the correct number of stairs Eeva has climbed.

Because $\frac{15}{25}=\frac{3\times5}{5\times5}$

Hence, $\frac{15}{25}$ is equivalent to $\frac{3}{5}$.

29. *(b)* To find the total tomatoes in each bunch and tomatoes left out divide 795 by 35.

$$\begin{array}{r} 35\overline{)\,795\,}(22 \\ -70\downarrow \\ \hline \times 95 \\ -70 \\ \hline 25 \end{array}$$

So, total number of tomatoes in each bunch (Q) = 22 and total number of tomatoes in left out (R) = 25

Hence, option (b) is correct.

30. *(a)* Total weight $= 64 + 1\frac{1}{4}$ of 64

$$= 64 + \frac{5}{4}\times 64 = 64 + 80 = 144 \text{ kg}$$

31. *(a)* According to the question,

 = 5 men and  = 7 women

Total  in the city = 6 × 5 = 30 men

Total  in the city = 5 × 7 = 35 women

∴ Required difference = 35 − 30 = 5

So, 5 women are more than men in the city.

Hence, option (a) is correct.

32. *(d)* Given time = 6 : 20 am

Time taken in going from home to school
= 45 min

Time taken in going from school to garden
= 18 min

∴ Time taken in going from home to garden
= (45 + 18) min = 63 min

So, time at which Michael will reach garden
= 6 : 20 am + 63 min = 7 : 23 am

33. *(c)* According to the question,

Sum of numbers in both the diagonals is equal.

Diagonals numbers have been connected by arrows.

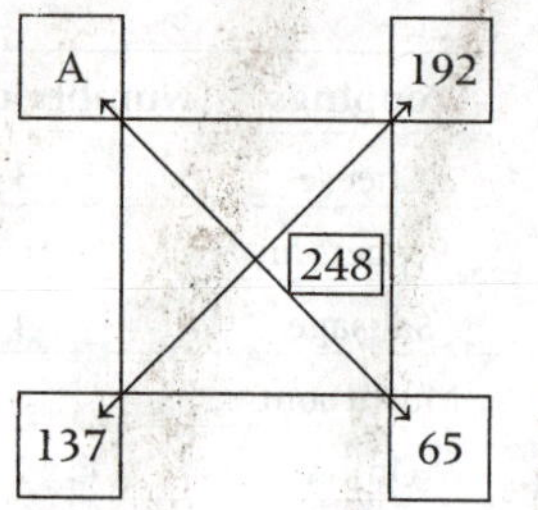

$$192 + 248 + 137 = A + 248 + 65$$
$$\Rightarrow \quad 577 = A + 313$$
$$\Rightarrow \quad A = 577 - 313 = 264$$

34. *(d)* Perimeter of folded napkin

$= 30 + 35 + 22 + 8 + 6 + 29 = 130$ cm

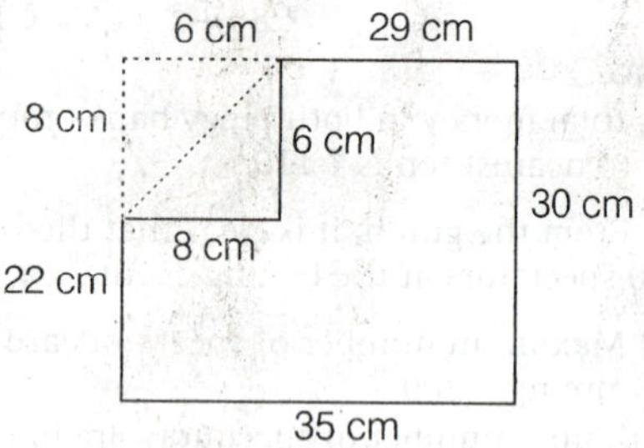

∴ Perimeter of unfolded napkin
$= 2(30+35) = 2\times65 = 130$ cm

So, required difference $= 130$ cm $- 130$ cm
$= 0$ cm

35. *(b)*

Days	Number of Oranges sold
Monday	$4\times4=16$
Tuesday	$6\times4=24$
Wednesday	$3\times4=12$
Thursday	$2\times4=8$
Friday	$7\times4=28$
Saturday	$3\times4=12$
Sunday	$1\times4=4$

Total number of oranges sold on Friday = 28

Total number of oranges sold in a week
$= 16 + 24 + 12 + 8 + 28 + 12 + 4 = 104$

∴ Required fraction $= \frac{28}{104} = \frac{7}{26}$